Pr
High-Impa

"There is no question that constantly seeking mentors and working to be one when you can breathes life into all of us. That's the 'why' for many. In *High-Impact Mentoring*, Bert and Sherry go deep to make sure each of us knows 'how' to be in a mentoring relationship more efficiently and impactfully. This book is a full-blown road map on mentoring, and I couldn't recommend it more highly!"

—Don Yaeger, eleven-time *New York Times*
best-selling author and speaker

"Bert Thornton has written a superb book on mentorship that is perfect for our times. While his advice is based on his career in the restaurant/hospitality business, I conclude from my experience in higher education, nonprofit management, and consulting for large civil projects, it is pertinent for all sectors. This advice is based on a singular belief that everyone deserves a chance to rise to their potential, and in doing so, the enterprise itself will grow and become better for it."

—Dr. G. Wayne Clough, author;
former president of the Georgia Institute of Technology;
former secretary of the Smithsonian Institution

"Mentoring changes lives. But we typically approach it without focus, strategy, or metrics. In this book, Sherry Hartnett provides a strategic road map for mentoring that matters. She shares insights built on in-depth research and real-world success stories from high-performance organizations. This book will forever shift your approach to mentoring, equipping you to make an extraordinary difference in the lives of others."

—Brett Culp, acclaimed
filmmaker and keynote speaker

"Finally, a book on the subject of mentoring has been written that comprehensively covers the topic from concept to reality. There is no more effective way to influence other individuals and no more important legacy than to personally invest in others. This book gives great insights and practical instruction on effective mentoring. Readers will elevate their mentoring effectiveness, which will result in positive impacts on countless lives."

—Mark Faulkner, president and CEO of
Baptist Health Care

"The old silverback mentor, Bert Thornton, has once again shown why he was so successful in his role mentoring young aspiring executives in the Waffle House organization. As he describes his methods for which he is known, he lays out his formula for the mentor and mentee in plain, practical, commonsense language in *High-Impact Mentoring*. It is a book that we all wish we had when we were young, but now teaches us why and how to pass along those fruitful lessons of experience to others."

—Sonny Perdue, former governor of Georgia
and connoisseur of Bert's Chili

"When asked who is an example of an extraordinary leader, I always note Sherry Hartnett. Her passion for mentoring entrepreneurs, young professionals, and emerging community leaders has had a direct positive impact on her community and our state. I highly recommend this book for any individual or organization that is looking to elevate themselves, establish a high-performing culture, and become more innovative in this twenty-first century environment."

—Karen B. Moore, CEO and founder of
Moore Communications Group

"For 95 percent of Bert's education and beyond in his career, I've been with him. He's a masterful learner and has captured the lessons from his experience in a wonderful way. Whether you want to be successful personally or lead an organization successfully, the 'how to' is all here. Life, family, and career are journeys. This road map, if followed, will lead you to your destination."

—Joe W. Rogers Jr., chairman of Waffle House,
Inc. (and, more importantly, Bert's friend)

"Not only a fantastic, comprehensive guidebook for anyone seeking to become an effective mentor but also a superb road map for success in business and life."

—Michelle K. Gallagher, director of
community engagement for Delta Air Lines, Inc.

"Want to change lives and prepare young adults for successful careers and lives? Here is a proven step-by-step guide for creating a high-impact mentoring program at your university or organization that connects emerging leaders with successful executives through enriching mentor and mentee experiences. Bert and Sherry outline the why and how of an executive mentoring program and provide proven, practical advice for developing tomorrow's leaders, enriching your organization, and creating value in other people's lives."

—Dr. Edward Ranelli, dean emeritus and
professor at the University of West Florida

"Simply put, Bert gives actionable and practical guidance for the guides themselves. The guidance is as solid and dependable as a Waffle House opening after a hurricane. Through his lifetime of business leadership excellence, followed by decades of experience as a mentor to some of the greatest business leaders of the last few generations, Bert has set forth in this short and actionable guide the distilled wisdom of what it takes to be the best mentor possible. Mentors now have a quick-witted and entertaining guide to follow rather than mentoring through happenstance. Your mentees deserve the best out of you, and this guide shows you how to deliver it."

—J. Alistair McKenzie, Florida trial attorney
and entrepreneur

"Sherry lays out the whys and hows of having a successful mentoring program. More importantly, she shares the proven tools to maximize the benefits of the mentoring relationship for mentors and mentees. Having the pleasure of working with Sherry, I can attest that she practices what she preaches, and the College of Business at UWF greatly benefits."

—Dr. Richard M. Fountain, dean of the
College of Business at the University of West Florida

"As the president and former chief leadership development officer at the Studer Community Institute, I recognize the value and importance of skill development training. Investing in human capital has a proven return on investment, with a multiplier effect. I can say without a doubt that mentoring is the single biggest accelerant for anyone interested in growth and professional success. Bert Thornton has perfected a process that gives both mentors and mentees the blueprint for maximizing the experience. This book is one of a kind and will be an invaluable tool for employees, leaders, and companies interested in a mentoring system that works to accelerate performance."

—Rachael Gillette, president of Studer
Community Institute

"High-Impact Mentoring offers practical, specific, and proven guidance for the new mentor and the veteran. It will be the 'go-to' for mentors across fields and across experience levels. Not only does it prepare leaders to be great mentors, it also supports leaders as they continue to grow and reflect on their own professional and personal practices."

—Dr. Katherine Kelbaugh, executive director
of the Museum School of Avondale Estates; executive director of the
National Association of Museum Schools

"High-Impact Mentoring is an inspiring book for both the novice and the expert mentor. Bert Thornton outlines an essential mentoring road map and guidelines for initiating, developing, and sustaining important relationships. He summarizes the business needs for mentors, while educating readers on the impact they can have on the future of their company, their mentees, and ultimately their continued individual growth."

—Marti Walsh, senior marketing director at
Fortune 500 companies

"This book provides comprehensive, step-by-step guidance for starting and optimizing a mentorship program. Superb! Professional development is so important in today's fast-paced and technology-driven environments, so any success metric starts with your best talent. If relationships are at the heart of business success, then this book presents a thoughtful and motivational road map for activating on the pillars of mentorship. This isn't about a training exercise. It's about realizing the reward that comes by creating a thriving, interactive culture of lifelong learners who want to excel and add value every day. That's high impact indeed—don't hesitate to read, learn, and go!"

—Michael G. Kane, COO, local markets,
LOCALiQ/USA TODAY NETWORK

"Bert Thornton and I were football teammates under the legendary Coach Bobby Dodd at Georgia Tech. Coach Dodd created a culture of excellence that was reflected in his students' performance, in the classroom and on the field. Bert's treasure of a book, *High-Impact Mentoring*, offers his readers the tools to do the same in a business context. His incredible attention to detail and his insistence that 'leadership always finds a way' ignite and organize the inner sparks we need to be great mentors."

—Bill Curry, author; speaker; 10-year NFL
center with the Green Bay Packers, Baltimore Colts, Houston Oilers,
and Los Angeles Rams (three Super Bowl rings); former head football
coach at Georgia Tech, Alabama, Kentucky, and Georgia State

"Mentoring is an investment in the future. Every moment spent developing a member of your team will strengthen the entire enterprise. Remember, business is a 'weak link' sport; it requires everyone to contribute at their peak. Sherry and Bert know this and make implementation simple. Using their tools and process, you ultimately will promote excellence, leverage strengths, correct weaknesses, raise the standards, drive growth, and, by the way, increase profits. Follow their lead!"

—Matt Eversmann, retired U.S. Army Ranger;
professional public speaker; hero of the epic film *Black Hawk Down* and
the Battle of Mogadishu; coauthor of *The Battle of Mogadishu* and *Walk
in My Combat Boots*

"This is the perfect sequel to *Find an Old Gorilla*. The book lives up to its subtitle of being a 'practical' guide to mentoring and is inspirational for potential mentors. I was amazed at how much the book reminded me of the people who have guided me in the past and kindled a fire in me to be there for others."

—Scott Remington, president and managing
shareholder of Clark Partington Law Firm

"I've not only been witness to Bert's incredible ability to mentor in an impactful way, I'm fortunate to say I've felt the direct impact of Bert's time, energy, and mentoring expertise on my life. He agreed to meet a 32-year-old at a Waffle House—an unseasoned business rookie with an idea—and willingly provided insight, tactics, and guidance, and inspired me to continue this journey. This idea of opening Perfect Plain Brewing Co. in Pensacola, FL, now has grown to four locations and 40+ employees in three years. I wouldn't have had the confidence to do it without him, and through that time, he continues to be one of the most influential mentors in my life, helping me both chase ideas and leave behind those not-so-good ones.

"Still today, as chief entrepreneur officer at a local entrepreneurial incubator in Pensacola, I continue to receive guidance from Bert and *High-Impact Mentoring* as I help others follow their journey to open their own small business.

"He knows how to impact lives, CEOs, and businesses of every shape and size. I'm confident that *High-Impact Mentoring* will help you do the same."

—D.C. Reeves, CEO and cofounder of Perfect
Plain Brewing Co.; chief entrepreneur officer at The Spring; author of
The Microbrewery Handbook

"One of the most important business gems is the power of being positive and encouraging, yet serious about results. Bert Thornton illustrates this in his life and in his writings.

"My company has grown tenfold in the past five years. Bert started mentoring me at the ground floor and advised me on everything from securing intellectual property (we had to fight a billion-dollar company to secure the trademark on our name), to landing deals, to growing the team.

"Today iFOLIO® powers brands including Madison Square Garden, the Atlanta Falcons, Andrews Institute, iD Tech, Equifax, the New York Knicks, and 5,350 paid users to connect, engage, and convert with digital marketing and patented analytics. iFOLIO helps people from sixth grade students, to college athletes, to mid-level business leaders, to the lieutenant governor of Georgia tell their story visually with digital communications. We delivered 204,000,000 seconds of engagement for our clients in all 50 U.S. states and 100 countries in the last 12 months.

"The industry average is eight seconds.

"There is power in investing in people and building a culture that is intentional, yet systematic. Every Friday, we have a team meeting that starts with the team's sharing stories from the week from living our core values: customer first, team over self, glass half-full, bias to action, and focus on results. Many of the team members who lead that meeting started at the company in our intern program and have been mentored to high levels of responsibility. People, relationships, and the culture you build make the difference in every season.

"Bert Thornton's insights on high-impact mentoring are invaluable for any executive looking to achieve both the next level and a legacy."

—Jean Marie Richardson, founding CEO and
president of iFOLIO

"*High-Impact Mentoring* is a splendid book by Bert Thornton and Dr. Sherry Hartnett. Who better to turn to for advice about mentoring than Bert, a Georgia Tech football standout, a U.S. Army artillery officer in Vietnam, longtime president of Waffle House, and, not in the least, the maestro of 'Bert's Chili' there. Clearly, Bert is a leader, but his real passion is mentoring. And having a passion, an enthusiasm, is key with Bert, in both mentors and especially in mentees.

"Bert's first book was *Find an Old Gorilla*, that is, an experienced leader who can best guide you through the paths in the jungle of life. Bert says not everyone can be a good mentor or a good mentee, but when the two hit it off, real benefits can accrue on both sides. The book is an eloquent extension of his first book. His many examples show that self-awareness and humility are better paths than arrogance and the 'my way or the highway' approach.

"One example Bert offers is about Florida businessman Quint Studer, whose tireless quest to help others does not involve seeking credit for himself. Agreeing with Bert, Studer is quoted as saying, 'The mentoring relationship can spark tremendous growth in both parties.'

"Another example of mentoring involved a Waffle House server who dropped a plate of dishes in front of a customer who happened to be singing star Merle Haggard. The woman was so embarrassed she told Bert she couldn't go back and serve him again. Bert told her to get ahold of herself and go right back out and serve him. She did and she and Haggard became friends.

"Bert himself says, 'To me, true success is about adding value—and the most meaningful place to add value is to another human being's life.' Always put people first, he says. Attitude, passion, energy, and the ability to communicate are crucial to the equation. And yes, be on time."

—Andrew Kilpatrick, author of *Of Permanent Value: The Story of Warren Buffett*

"I have been blessed with Bert in my life directly as a mentor. He truly cares about adding value and believes the best way is by adding value to someone else's life. Bert does the work; he doesn't just talk the talk. If you can find someone to emulate and save time implementing lessons they've already learned, why wouldn't you do it? It is wonderful that he and Sherry have teamed up so others can benefit from *High-Impact Mentoring* and the lessons within."

—Olevia McNally, director of telemedicine practice development at Envision Physician Services

HIGH-IMPACT
Mentoring

HIGH-IMPACT
Mentoring

*A Practical Guide to Creating
Value in Other People's Lives*

BERT THORNTON
DR. SHERRY HARTNETT

BOOKLOGIX˙
Alpharetta, GA

ISBN: 978-1-6653-0344-6 - Paperback
ISBN: 978-1-6653-0345-3 - eBook

Library of Congress Control Number: 2021920872

Printed in the United States of America   1 0 1 2 2 1

⊗ This paper meets the requirements of ANSI/NISO Z39.48-1992 (Permanence of Paper)

Photo of Bert Thornton courtesy of the Georgia Tech Alumni Association

My portion of this book is dedicated to all the unsung heroes: the legion of anonymous mentors out there who go about doing, every day, all the work necessary to sustain success for their families and themselves—and then, in what would have been their spare time, work hard to help create tremendous value in other people's lives…just because they believe it is the right thing to do.

—Bert Thornton

To my sons, Jake and Brad: May they be blessed with the wisdom of good mentors and be great mentors to others.

—Dr. Sherry Hartnett

CONTENTS

FOREWORD

One thing I've come to appreciate in the course of my life is the value of learning from others. I've met people from many fields and organizations, with various job titles and levels of leadership. I've learned from all of them. And I've found most successful individuals have this in common: They know how important it is to seek out and pay attention to the wisdom of those who came before them.

When you ask really successful people, "What is the one piece of advice you'd give someone who is trying to launch a big career or start a small business?" they almost always say, "Get a mentor right away." This may be the single biggest differentiator between success and failure. Having a mentor early on helps you avoid big mistakes that might slow you down, cost a lot of money, and maybe even cause you to quit. It can also help you spot opportunities you wouldn't have seen otherwise.

Sometimes people tell me their biggest mistake was not finding a mentor early enough. People may think they're not "ready" for a mentor, as they are just starting out or they may think people won't be willing to help them. Neither is true. The earlier you seek out a mentor, the better off you'll be. And most people are not just willing to help, they're happy and excited to be asked.

I am a huge believer in the value of mentoring in growing small businesses. In fact, when we were trying to create an entrepreneurial ecosystem in Pensacola, one of the first things we did was to get a formal mentoring program in place. It was a vital foundation piece. We ended up creating The Spring Venture Mentoring Service (VMS).

This program is based on the model used by the renowned VMS program at the Massachusetts Institute of Technology. The Spring VMS offers confidential team mentoring services to entrepreneurs across our community. Carefully selected mentors from various backgrounds volunteer their time to help local business owners grow thriving companies. It's a great program and, so far, has been really successful.

When we were getting VMS set up, we knew right away Bert was a natural fit for the program. I had read his first book, *Find an Old Gorilla*, and he was legendary for mentoring in the community and had an incredible reputation. It was clear to see he had a huge passion for giving back, and mentorship was the perfect vehicle. He has all the qualities we were looking for and knows how to articulate and teach them to others.

Recently I read an article titled "Why Mentoring Matters: A Conversation with Carlos Lejnieks." (Lejnieks) Carlos is a leader of the Newark, New Jersey-based chapter of Big Brothers Big Sisters of America. Not only does he oversee the mentoring of over 1,000 school-age children, he himself is a mentoring success story. In the 1990s, he was a high school dropout, but mentors started him on a journey that ended up leading him to Brown University, Goldman Sachs, and the London School of Economics and Political Science.

Carlos says mentoring is a life thing, not just a job thing. It helps create stability and an overall feeling that you are cared for. Sometimes just feeling valued and knowing that someone cares is a game changer. A little support from a mentor can make a big difference for someone in a tough situation. He says good mentors see qualities in people that they may not even realize they have and help draw them out.

When I read this article, I realized it's exactly the kind of mentoring and impact Bert Thornton provides in our community. In the process, he helps change the trajectories of people's lives. So when he asked me to write the foreword to *High-Impact Mentoring*, I was honored to do it. And the fact that Dr. Sherry Hartnett wrote the second half of the book made it even better. I know her from her work at the University of West Florida, where I am the entrepreneur-in-residence. I felt the two of them together would create an incredible book.

Also, I am convinced the time is right for this book. Mentoring is a very old practice; in fact, its roots are thought to reach back to Ancient Greece. Yet lately I am seeing a resurgence of interest in mentoring. This makes perfect sense to me. In the intro, Bert gives some of the reasons why.

He talks about the complexity and chaos of the external environment; the pace at which business moves and technology advances; the cultural, demographic, and political shifts taking place; and more. Businesses have to be agile and adaptable, and that means everyone must be at the top of their game. Add in the lean training budgets many companies have and the need for ongoing learning in general, and you can see there is kind of a "perfect storm" of factors that make mentoring not just a "nice-to-have" but a "must-have."

And it is not just a matter of older, more experienced employees sharing knowledge with younger ones. Like Bert, I am a huge fan of reverse mentoring. People of all ages and stages have something we can learn from each other. Younger people can not only help more seasoned executives make sense of technology, they truly help us understand issues like unconscious bias and the need for true inclusion.

For all of these reasons, you will appreciate this book. Bert gives all sorts of practical "across the table" advice on how to be a great mentor, what to look for in a mentee, how to establish a strong relationship up front, and so on. He blends nuts-and-bolts business advice with deeper life insights to share with the mentee. (I love what he says about how it's better to start with a sense of purpose and a set of goals than wander aimlessly until a "stone in your shoe" forces you to make a change. This is a great analogy on taking an offensive versus a defensive approach to life.)

Sherry's part of the book is also incredibly valuable. She lays out step-by-step how to create a formal mentoring program inside an organization. She walks the reader through the process of figuring out what they want the program to accomplish, to finding the right champion, to setting goals, to matching up mentees and mentors, and more. She gives a nice blueprint to help you create a program that works, prove its value to shareholders and decision-makers, and nurture it and keep it going over time.

Bert and Sherry bring together the best of two different worlds. When you read *High-Impact Mentoring*, you will get excited about being a mentor yourself, creating a program inside your own organization, or possibly both.

This book makes it clear that being a mentor is so, so rewarding. I often think about the phrase "Who is helping whom?" If you're not a mentor and you have some knowledge and experience to share, please do. You will never regret the relationships you form, the good feeling of helping someone get a foothold in their career, and the surprise of seeing, once again, that even the oldest "gorilla" still has more to learn.

—Quint Studer

Lejnieks, Carlos, Bill Javetski, Dana Sand. "Why Mentoring Matters: A Conversation with Carlos Lejnieks." April 1, 2021, Interview, *McKinsey Accelerate*, McKinsey & Company.

Why Now Is the Right Time for Mentoring

The world has never needed mentors more than we do right now. We started working on this book well before COVID-19, and both of us firmly believed that statement then. Now, as the world struggles to regain some equilibrium in the wake of the pandemic, we're even more convinced of the value of mentorship. Between the two of us, we've served as mentors, been mentees ourselves, and helped others become mentors and mentees—and these experiences have positively changed our lives. And we believe mentorship has a tremendous role to play in building strong, resilient companies and organizations.

The world has been in chaos and upheaval for a long time now, and the pace of change is increasing. You may have heard the term "VUCA," which stands for Volatility, Uncertainty, Complexity, and Ambiguity. This acronym has been kicked around for decades, which only goes to show we've *needed* it for decades. It's a trendy, managerial way of saying, "What the heck is going on out there? And what's going to happen next?"

The answer is, "No one really knows." In a world of rapidly advancing technology; shifting global alliances; and political, cultural, and social upheaval, how could we? The future is a moving target. The job of a leader today is to try to find patterns in the chaos and take the action that makes the most sense for the short-term. (Needless to say, long-term planning has been on the side-line for a while now.)

As impactful as the pandemic is, it's just another variation on the theme that's been playing out for decades. *Change is the only constant.* The only way a business can survive is by being agile and adaptable. We must be able to make quick, smart decisions in the face of uncertainty. We must develop a leadership team and a culture that lend themselves to making constant adjustments. At times we may have to sharply pivot and go in a new direction. This is just the way business is now, and it isn't likely to change.

To navigate this ongoing chaos requires the right mindset and skillset. Everyone inside a company must be willing and able to continuously learn (and just as important, *unlearn* what they thought they knew). This requires a lot of self-awareness and humility. It also means we must consciously create a culture that encourages people to master and live by the "soft skills" we hear so much about: critical thinking; emotional intelligence; creativity; and the ability to connect, communicate, and collaborate with others on the team.

This is where mentorship comes in. Organizations must encourage and promote mentorship because no one is born with the skills needed to lead and work in today's business environment (or, any business environment, for that matter). We need role models, teachers, and coaches to show us the way. That's what mentors are. In *A Game Plan for Life: The Power of Mentoring*, Don Yaeger's excellent book with Coach John Wooden, Don points out, "It's not enough to set about finding a mentor; it's every bit as important to concentrate on becoming one yourself." But, great mentorship doesn't "just happen." Individuals must make a conscious choice to become mentors and learn how best to do so.

Before we break down some of the benefits effective mentorship brings to today's world, let's take a quick look at the different forms it embodies:

One-on-one mentoring: This is the traditional mentoring model. One mentor and one mentee begin a mentoring relationship in which the mentor has more experience in the mentee's area of interest. The main goal of the relationship is to help the mentee develop skills, improve, and continually achieve.

Peer mentoring: This mentoring style involves colleagues in the same age group. They take turns acting as mentor and mentee. Overall, peer mentors create a formal support system of accountability and learning.

Group mentoring: In this style of mentoring, one mentor works with a group of mentees. This is beneficial because it allows many mentees to learn at the same time.

Reverse mentoring: This occurs when a more junior person mentors a more senior person. Reverse mentoring is tremendously valuable in helping "seasoned" leaders and employees learn about technology, social media, diversity and inclusion, and so forth. It can help you move your culture to one that's more inviting to younger talent.

A Silver Bullet for Struggling Organizations?

Whatever form it takes, mentoring can help us successfully manage some of the big issues today's companies, leaders, and employees face. You might even call it a "silver bullet" solution. Of course, great mentorship doesn't exist in a vacuum. For it to work to its full potential, an organization must have viable products and services, a good strategy, and above all, consistently great leadership. But a well-planned, well-executed mentorship program can benefit even struggling organizations in surprisingly powerful ways. For example:

Mentoring sharpens a company's ability to execute. It goes without saying that companies must be agile, fast-thinking, and fast-acting if they're to survive. By sharing their years of accumulated wisdom, mentors help people broaden their perspective, cut through the information overload and "noise" flying at them from all directions, and get to the heart of what matters. When we aren't bogged down in extraneous details, we can move quickly and purposefully.

A solid mentoring program can help us deal with training budget shortfalls... Quite often in times of economic turmoil (like now), training budgets are on the chopping block. Mentors play a huge role in transferring knowledge and vital skills. They are a great source of on-the-job training that costs very little. (On a related note, when a new employee is assigned a mentor early on, they're more likely to hit the ground running. This is important in a world that moves at lightning speed.)

...and it sets the stage for the ongoing learning that will be needed in the future. Increasingly, we need our employees to have a "just-in-time" skillset. The education system can't keep up, and companies will need to ramp up their training to bridge the skills gap. Mentors will likely play a vital role in helping employees perform well while they integrate new learnings.

It helps attract and retain talent. For obvious reasons, companies need a strong team of employees, and it's just as crucial that, once hired, good people stay with us. A mentoring program shows them there's a path for advancement inside our company. Millennials, in particular, deeply value training and development. By sharing their knowledge and experience with younger employees, mentors help them grow and progress. At the same time, they teach younger people how to navigate challenges specific to their workplace so they are less likely to leave. (Remember, people don't quit their job; they quit their boss.)

It helps new employees hit the ground running a lot faster. We no longer have the luxury of long onboarding periods as new employees. The pace of business requires everyone to become a contributing member of the team almost immediately. Mentoring can help expedite progress for a new employee.

Mentoring helps engage employees. Mentoring makes it more likely that people will "lean in" to their work. They're being challenged to learn new things so they don't become complacent. They have a chance to prove themselves and use their skills and talents in new ways. They may become a wellspring of new ideas. They feel invested in and valued. All of this sparks their passion and energy for their work and shores up their commitment to the company.

It helps people build the relationship skills today's companies need to survive. Strong relationships—based on honesty, trust, transparency, and empathy—matter more than ever now. Truly, companies must be masters at innovation, collaboration, and teamwork. All of these things hinge on our ability to foster strong relationships. Mentoring builds relationships in two ways. First, the mentor/mentee relationship creates a strong bond as it evolves. But also, both parties apply the skills they learn in the process to other relationships.

It helps our people weather tough storms. COVID has put incredible stress on leaders and employees. In fact, many organizations have moved beyond stress and into the realm of trauma. By putting things in perspective ("We've lived through other hard times and survived"), providing a safe space for mentees to vent about their stresses and struggles, and sharing coping skills, mentors can go a long way toward helping employees build resilience and ease loneliness and isolation.

Mentoring helps organizations become more diverse and inclusive. There is a huge focus right now on these issues. In many organizations, older employees may need to learn how best to work with those from different racial and cultural backgrounds, belief systems, and orientations. This is where reverse mentoring shines. But actually, any type of mentoring that puts people from different age groups together helps create more diverse, inclusive workplaces. The more folks from different generations get to know each other and have meaningful exchanges, the more we break down barriers…and the more unified we become.

Mentorship Is Valuable in Both Good Times and Hard Times

We've been talking about mentoring in the context of how it can help companies navigate times of crisis or great change and survive. But mentoring has many benefits in "normal" times too. (We put "normal" in quotation marks for a reason. What we are really talking about is those relatively smooth times we sometimes get between crises!) In good times or tough times, mentoring has benefits that apply to all parties.

Obviously, mentoring helps employees in countless ways. They meet professional goals faster. They learn where their blind spots are, which helps them avoid pitfalls and know where to improve. They learn to recognize opportunities they otherwise might have missed. Thanks to the mentor's social capital, they get a leg up in networking and building connections. Quite often the real gift mentors give isn't the knowledge they pass on; it's the sense of optimism they inspire. We don't need to tell you that what's good for your employees is good for your company!

But mentoring benefits the "givers" of knowledge as much as the receivers. The relationship is a reciprocal one. Mentors often learn as much as they teach. As you work with the mentee, you will need to take a step back and ponder what you really "know." This introspection will either reinforce your viewpoint or change it, driving learning and personal growth. Besides, mentoring is a form of giving back—and giving back feels good.

Very often, mentoring relationships last a lifetime. They don't end just because someone changes roles or companies. These relationships endure and continue to benefit both parties.

Finally, mentoring relationships transcend business. Whether we're mentors or mentees, these relationships enrich our personal lives, too. There is no sharp divide between "work" and "home"—or at least, there shouldn't be. As we grow as leaders and employees, we also grow as spouses, partners, parents, friends, and neighbors.

Please read on to discover some of the core attributes that make a great mentor. These are truths we have learned throughout our careers and lives. Then, keep reading to discover a proven formula for creating a successful mentoring program inside your organization.

It's a wonderful thing to realize the work we do is more than a way to make a great living. It's a way to make a great life. And the realization that we can have a positive influence on others in our sphere—guiding them to become better employees, leaders, and human beings in the face of increasingly challenging times—may be the greatest gift mentoring brings us.

—Bert Thornton

—Dr. Sherry Hartnett

BERT'S ADVICE

Why Does This Book Exist ...and Who Can Benefit from It?

Dear Organizational Leader:

Thank you for reading this book! Before we get started, I'd like to ask, and answer, a question: *Why did I write a book like this?* For the long answer, I refer you back to our Introduction, "Why Now Is the Right Time for Mentoring." The short answer to the question is simply that there is nothing else out there like this book.

There are no other practical, step-by-step, how-to guides for sitting down with rising high achievers or emerging leaders and successfully helping them create value in their own lives. Further, from a business perspective, there is no solid, competent, definitive advice out there for the CEO, university official, or organizational leader who realizes the immense value of a culture of mentorship and wants to successfully infuse one into his or her organization.

The books Sherry Hartnett and I have seen about mentoring generally fall into one of three categories:

- A laborious study of all things mentoring from the beginning of time
- Cute little books that tell stories about fictional people like Jack and Susie who take great advice and live happily ever after
- Good books that are interesting to read but not specific enough to be of great value when trying to maximize the value of a specific mentoring relationship

Imagine reading a book about the history of boxing or a fun story about a boy from the Bronx who got a shot at the title…and then you climb into the ring for a real match with an experienced boxer who actually knows what he's doing. Not good. So, for my part in this effort, I did not write to entertain. I wrote to explain. I wrote to offer you real-world observations and solutions that have passed the test of time. This book is a practical guide for high-impact, face-to-face, "do this, don't do that" mentoring.

When I became president and chief operations officer at Waffle House, I realized in order to meet our growth goals, we would need a great deal of fresh talent and an effective system to maximize their development. Training someone to do a task is easy. Developing an aspiring person to his or her full potential requires dedicated leaders who are willing to share their wisdom, knowledge, and experience through a program that systematically governs that process.

Ships don't "drift" into port, and emerging talent won't "drift" into senior leadership positions. Well-intended random mentoring efforts won't work. Systems work, and systems sustain. The need I felt for an effective mentoring platform and the tremendous opportunity to create a system to transform so much raw potential into successful producers became my passion. In the following five years at Waffle House, we quadrupled the ranks of our middle and senior leadership potential.

A few years ago, I published *Find an Old Gorilla*, a well-received leadership book written from the mentee's perspective. It is a guide to help rising high achievers determine where they are in life and business, what they really want (which may not be what they think they want), and how to find the right people to help get them there. *Find an Old Gorilla* also touched on the basic laws of success and offered a study of the successful leadership model: specifically, what successful leaders do and don't do, what they think about and don't think about. It was a "self-mentoring in a box" resource and also a bridge between mentee and mentor, giving them a place to start together and a great deal to talk about.

High-Impact Mentoring is a natural follow-up. It speaks directly to the leadership parties in the mentor/mentee relationship.

Part 1 ("Bert's Advice") speaks directly to the executive mentor. It is a practical guide offering practical advice on how to successfully and comprehensively evaluate the mentee before you and most effectively guide him or her into and through the "success lanes" of business and life.

No doubt, being a good mentor takes hard work. Like everything else, if you want to do it well, you have to check three boxes:

- You must want to do it.
- You must know how to do it.
- You must have the ability to do it.

My part in this book is to help you check boxes number two and three. I am hoping that, in the process of reading it, you'll also get all the information and confidence you need to check box number one: to *want* to tackle the job of guiding and inspiring the mentee across the table from you to great success.

There is no doubt that a successful mentoring relationship can positively change a life. Just as certainly, a well-executed mentoring program can absolutely have the same positive impact on a company. But where is the definitive advice on how to build that culture in a large organization? It's in Part 2 of *High-Impact Mentoring* ("Sherry's Advice").

In Part 2, the best of the best in this category, Dr. Sherry Hartnett advises the corporate or higher education leader on how she created and installed the large, hands-on, immensely successful mentoring program at the University of West Florida in Pensacola. This is a program that carefully matches a legion of savvy area business and organizational leaders with rising college stars and recent graduates and then goes on to successfully nurture those mutually effective mentoring relationships. I've seen a number of college and corporate mentoring programs. In my opinion, Sherry's is by far the best for all the reasons she outlines in Part 2 of this book.

If you are that large organization leader contemplating your own mentoring program, please pay close attention. Attempting to install an excellent, large mentoring program without studying and following Sherry's "Seven-Step Process" might be like trying to build a beautiful building without a set of blueprints.

So, one more thing…

In one of his outstanding *Pensacola News Journal* leadership articles, Florida businessman and philanthropist Quint Studer carefully points out that, "The mentoring relationship can spark tremendous growth in both parties. Great mentors know they are not finished products, and often they learn as much from the mentee as the mentee learns from them." (Studer)

So, the bonus in mentoring is two-fold: One, we learn when we teach, and two, we feel wonderful when we help other people. I have found that my happiest friends are not the ones who play the most golf or take the most cruises. The folks who seem to be having the most fun lead a life of gratitude for what they have, and they express this gratitude through reciprocation—their sincere efforts to give back, especially to deserving young, emerging leaders.

How wonderful that an emerging leader, under your direction, can grow straight and strong—can absorb your knowledge and experience without taking on many of the scars you earned as you fought your way through the jungles of business and life, by yourself.

How awesome that the successful mentoring program you initiate and drive will so positively impact the rising stars in your organization!

—Bert Thornton

P.S. Before we get into the practical advice, I have an instructive parable to share. Turn the page and you will find an illustrating sequel to the parable encountered in *Find an Old Gorilla*. I hope you will enjoy it!

Studer, Quint. "3 Major Traits of a Successful Leader (and How to Develop them)," *Pensacola News Journal*, Feb. 9, 2019.
https://www.pnj.com/story/money/business/2019/02/09/three-major-traits-successful-leader-and-how-develop-them/2807082002/

The Origins of MEN-TOR-SHIP

Once upon a time in a land far, far away, there lived a band of gorillas, young and old alike. These were not your average gorillas. These gorillas had developed extraordinary skills in the areas of communication, organization, community enhancement, and awareness of the need for ongoing development. They became famous in the land for building a vibrant community of extremely productive, effective, efficient, involved citizens.

The magnificence all started one day at a meeting of elders when Jefe, the chief of the gorilla band, announced there was a need to transfer the history and skills of the older generation to the band's emerging youth. This wise old gorilla realized that by doing so, he could accelerate the learning curve of the younger gorillas and save them many of the scars the older gorillas had inherited through wrong decisions.

In the gorilla language of the band, the word "MEN" meant "person," "TOR" was the word for "experience," and "SHIP" connoted "send, share, or give to." Consequently, Jefe decided to call the program "MEN-TOR-SHIP."

In one of his less-celebrated moves, Jefe decided to turn the whole program over to Blazer, a gorilla famous for his aggressive, "get it done" attitude but not particularly well known for thinking things through. True to form, Blazer's first order of business was to make the program mandatory for all gorillas in the band.

He was shocked to find that five old gorillas immediately proclaimed they did not have time for the program and three young gorillas wanted nothing to do with it. Undaunted, Blazer insisted that everyone participate and started putting together old and young gorillas for an experience-sharing relationship.

Blazer's next decision was even more disastrous than his first as he paired Thor, the great band warrior, with Aggie, who wanted to do absolutely nothing except be the best farmer in the land. He then matched Einstein, whose life vision was to be the great thinker and band leadership advisor, with Ali, the band's greatest athlete.

Blazer was amazed that the program went nowhere.

Jefe, returning to his senses, saw the problem and reassigned the effort to Sherilla, the great organizer. Sherilla weeded out the malcontents and then matched up young and old gorillas based on the younger's need, the older gorilla's ability to provide, and some common interests between the two.

The program was a resounding success with eager, deserving young gorillas rising to top ranks, helping create value in all areas of band life, and later even rejoining the program as givers rather than receivers.

The band's rise to greatness seemed to know no bounds, and it came to be known throughout the land by the two words of its gorilla language name, "WORLD," meaning "a great band," and "CLASS," meaning "high achievers."

And the aggressive-but-misassigned Blazer went on to become a great warrior...a job more suited to his gifts and more forgiving of his brawn-to-brain ratio.

CHAPTER 1

What It Takes to Be a Great Mentor (the Core Attributes)

What is a successful life? It's one of those philosophical questions with no "right" answer. Entire libraries could be written on the subject! My view is that a successful life isn't so much about accumulating wealth or power or adulation. To me, true success is about adding value—and the most meaningful place to add value is to another human being's life.

I believe mentoring—which I'll briefly define here as purposefully sharing your wisdom, knowledge, and experience with another individual who is ready to learn from you—is a wonderful way to do this.

Yet, while mentoring is a noble calling, it may not be for you. It's only one of many ways to help people in their pursuit of achievement. Sometimes just a kind word of encouragement or an expression of appreciation can be a great form of support. The trick is to find what kind of value-added support works for you.

I say this because Sherry and I agree: Mentoring is not meant for everybody. This implies nothing—good *or* bad—about a person. It is simply a reflection on desire and availability. Not everyone wants to be a mentor. Not everyone *should* be a mentor. Not everyone has time to be a mentor. As Sherry will point out later in this book, compulsory (conscripted) mentoring in a large organization may not only be ineffective but can actually be counterproductive.

To be effective in the mentor role requires a great deal of commitment. You must spend—or, more appropriately said, invest—plenty of time, not only in face-to-face meetings, whether physical or virtual and in phone calls, but also in research about your mentee and his or her areas of interest. It also involves reading and broadening your knowledge in order to offer good, solid, appropriate advice.

Of course, if you are simply going to sit down for a chat and suggest a few things to the person across the table, it's not necessary to go to all that trouble. But then, that's not mentoring. That's just friendly conversation, and it generates the same kind of random advice one can get at a cocktail party. Mentoring is about the self-sacrifice it takes to help create and build value in someone else's life. It's about the satisfaction and immense pleasure received in watching someone (your someone) learn, grow, achieve, and succeed...all because you took the time.

Take the time...and remember that your moments are other people's memories.

How Mentoring Shaped a Waffle House VP

This is a story about the tremendous potential of successful mentoring.

In the 1990s and well into my Waffle House career, I was in a constant search for fresh talent. I had heard a great deal about a brand-new unit manager named Dave Rickell who had made quite a name for himself as a manager trainee. He was a graduate of a premium college; an ex-athlete; and a hardworking, fine young man with great people skills.

Knowing I needed to meet this potential superstar, I visited Dave's restaurant early one evening when I knew he would be working during a supper shift. We worked together behind the counter bussing tables, washing dishes, and taking care of our customers for about an hour and then we moved into the back room to get to know each other better.

That is when Dave asked me the question that would change his life and his career, forever. He said, "Bert, how do I get promoted?" I told him, "It's very simple, Dave. You make yourself the obvious choice." What followed then was the first of many, many conversations over the years about what it takes to succeed in life and business.

Today, Dave Rickell is an operational executive vice president with Waffle House in charge of more than half of 1,900 restaurants in 25 states. The annual revenue line of his restaurants is an impressively large number, and on any given day, Dave has between 30,000 and 35,000 people working for him.

All of this success came from the fact that, at every step in his career, he asked, he listened, and he made himself the obvious choice. When someone has the "right stuff," they can go far in life—and being able to help them realize that potential is hugely rewarding!

There are five characteristics of a truly successful mentor:

1. **Gratitude for what you have and a sincere desire to reciprocate, to give back to the next generation of emerging leaders.** In the Bible, giving back is mentioned as being a part of the journey of faith. Luke 12:48 says, "For unto whomever much is

given, of him much shall be required." Virtually every religious tradition urges followers to share of their gifts and talents. Whatever your beliefs may be, if you feel a calling to serve others, you might have what it takes to be a mentor.

2. **A sincere interest in the mentee.** This calls into play the important need to select the right mentee. A perfect match for you is based upon:

- A good fit with your goals and interests
- A good fit with what the mentee needs versus what you offer
- Your excitement about the opportunity to create value in this person's life

3. **A track record of demonstrated success.** (If not, why would anyone listen?)

4. **Knowledge, interest, or expertise in the mentee's specific area of interest.**

5. **Peer respect.** (The greater the respect given the mentor by his or her peers, the greater the chances for the mentee's success.) Peer respect seems to be the ultimate litmus test for a successful mentor.

Some other mentor characteristics that will contribute to a mentee's success are:

- Availability/accessibility. Do you truly have time to work with the mentee?
- Tactfulness. The mentee is inexperienced and will make many missteps. Great mentors remember that they once wore those shoes, too. Be gentle and kind.
- Empathy and caring. If you don't truly care about the mentee and sincerely want him or her to succeed, the experience won't benefit either of you.

- Willingness to tell the truth. While it's important to be caring, it's also important to be ready to give the kind of feedback that's tough to hear.
- Patience. Give the mentee time to arrive at his or her own answers. Your job is not to jump in with solutions too soon. Growth can be slow, inconsistent, and inconvenient, and if you can't live with that, mentorship might be frustrating for you.
- Forgiveness. My friend Scott Remington is the president and managing shareholder at the Clark Partington law firm. Scott says his mentor, Bill Bond, compares training lawyers to training bird dogs. Bill, a sage gentleman whom everyone calls "Bubba," told him, "The young ones will chew things and pee on the carpet, but if you stick with them, the rewards are worth the pain." Scott's attitude is to forgive the mistakes and help his mentees learn from them.
- The ability to be a good listener. Great mentors don't do all the talking. They are just as good at listening. Good listeners help others clarify their thinking and build their self-esteem.
- "Common ground" with the mentee (in relation to interests or background). Sherry says this "jump-starts" the relationship.

Of course, this is not an exhaustive list. But it's a good start.

Quint Studer: The Epitome of a Great Mentor

A great (and rare) example of someone who possesses the entire slate of successful mentoring characteristics is Quint Studer. Quint is a Pensacola, Florida, businessman and philanthropist, and if there ever was anyone with a solid track record of success, it's him. Early on, Quint made history in the healthcare management arena by taking struggling hospitals from the bottom to the top in terms of success metrics. Quint is co-owner of the Minor League Baseball team the Pensacola Blue Wahoos—the Double-A affiliate of the Miami Marlins—as well as a number of other businesses. He has been the driving force in a tremendous revitalization of downtown Pensacola and works to help other communities across the U.S. reinvent themselves.

So how does Quint spend his spare time? Golf? Cruises? Not at all. Quint's tireless quest is helping others strive for improvement. In fact, he has written twelve books about making things better for people and communities, aimed at audiences from hospitals to cities to leaders at all levels in all types of organizations. His Studer Community Institute exists to this end, driving excellence in early learning, leadership development, civic awareness, and citizen contribution to community vibrancy.

Much of what Quint does in this regard goes unnoticed, because he doesn't care about accolades. His reward is in seeing things improve and watching organizations and individuals move from mediocre to excellent. That is his passion, and he excels at it. There is a long list of cities, hospitals, businesses, and business leaders who have been the beneficiaries of Quint's wisdom and willingness to share his time and treasure to advance them to a position of prominence.

This is what a great mentor does. He or she takes the knowledge gained and the peer respect acquired through great personal success and applies them in a sincere effort to help create value in other people and their endeavors. It doesn't get any better than that.

With regard to the larger executive mentoring program, Sherry will detail later many other essential qualifications regarding experience and networking ability.

For now, please ask yourself if you honestly feel you can check all or most of the boxes above. If you do, you have what it takes to find a rising star and help them become as successful as they can possibly be. If you don't, you should probably stop here. There are lots of other great ways to give back.

As I said earlier, mentoring one-on-one is not necessarily for everyone. It takes a certain kind of person. If you feel you are that person, read on. Mentoring is an amazing journey, and I hope you will decide it's the right one for you.

CHAPTER 2

What Makes a Good Mentee?

In the previous chapter, we discussed the skills and mindset you need to be a great mentor. But remember, this relationship is a two-way street. What's equally important is that the mentee has some essential characteristics that make mentoring him or her worth your time and effort.

That mentee must:

- Truly want to be mentored and be willing to be involved in the process
- Possess self-awareness, the desire to learn, and not feel that he or she already knows it all (It's what you learn after you know it all that counts!)
- Be open to your advice and feedback (although you must earn trust in that regard)
- Be unafraid to implement new learnings
- Have the capacity to perform at a higher level
- Display a strong work ethic

To quote Sherry, "Participation without passion is a recipe for failure." For the mentee to be successful in this relationship (or any other endeavor, for that matter), he or she must also have the "want to" (desire), the "can do" (ability), and the "know how to do" (knowledge). The above bullet list of "mentee musts" is the "want to" and the "can do." You will supply the "know how to do."

Realize that knowing how to be a good mentee is not intuitive (unless you have found a superstar). So, once you have picked the right mentee for you, some of the initial advice you may have to give is about his or her behavior in order to maximize the success of the relationship.

You may have to coach these important mentee responsibilities:

- Come prepared. Don't just show up for the meeting…prepare for it and own it. Impress your mentor. Take ownership of the relationship.
- Ask thoughtful questions (prepare them ahead of time).
- Be candid about everything: issues, problems, likes and dislikes, wants and aversions, what's working, what's not…
- Have good follow-through on assignments.
- Don't be afraid to call when something crazy comes up between meetings… (Sometimes mentees may hesitate to "bother" their mentor, so you need to make it clear that you want to hear from them anytime they need guidance.)
- However…make a good faith effort to solve problems on your own first. Consider bringing a solution or two to bounce off the mentor.

Please note: If your mentee is smart, they will learn everything they can about you. They should read articles about you, any articles you have written, and anything you have published. It may help if you send them some of these pieces so they can get a good sense of what you've accomplished and how you think. In fact, you might recommend some of your favorite leadership books so they can understand what resonates with you.

If teaching is "pitching" and learning is "catching," you may actually have to teach your mentee how to learn so they can catch what you are pitching.

Here is a good way to think about it. Learning on the part of the mentee is a process of:

- Deficit realization (knowing what you don't know)
- The drive to acquire skills (information, knowledge, ability)
- A sense of nagging curiosity (an underrated advantage)
- A willingness to put in the work (Saying is not doing, talking is not working, and having information is not executing!)
- A desire for constant growth

Keep in mind that if your mentee already knew this stuff, they wouldn't be sitting in front of you. Your challenge as the mentor is to nurture those learning skills and deliver a superstar.

All Mentees Are Not Created Equal (and That Brings Challenges)

It is also important to remember that mentees come in all ages and stages, and you need to be prepared to react appropriately. I have a theory about ages and stages that may be relevant to the mentor's challenge. The mentee's stage in life may impact his mindset and how he or she receives the information offered. This fact can affect the observant mentor's "pitching" style.

The following very general age/stage chart is just my opinion based on my observations over the years. Yes, it's somewhat stereotypical, and no, these descriptions may not be accurate for any given individual. Everyone is different, so take this in the spirit in which it's intended—with the proverbial grain of salt!

Ages and Stages of a Mentee

- **Late teens and early 20s.** Frequently (but certainly not always) this age group tends to think they have all the answers even though they haven't heard most of the questions yet. Sometimes this is just the mentor's perception and not how the young person intends to come across. Either way, you will have to earn their respect, personally, before they will listen. Quietly displayed energy and self-confidence on your part along with advice that resonates with the mentee and works for them earns this respect. What doesn't work is a "know-it-all" or "you-need-to-be-more-like-me" attitude. A good start on earning a young person's respect is to place yourself in their situation, their circumstances, or their dilemma. I tell people when someone is "hurting," you have to start "in the hurt." You have to start where they are, not where you are. You can't say, "Life is wonderful. I feel great! You should, too!" Empathy for their plight puts you on their side of the table, not across from it.

- **Mid to late 20s.** A crisis of confidence sets in. Suddenly, they realize they don't have all the answers. They wonder what life is really all about and what's in store for them in the future. Often at this age, people become much more receptive to mentoring!

- **The 30s.** This is "sponge time." These individuals are learning and acquiring skills rapidly. The successful ones are developing "street credit" with bosses and peers.

- **The 40s.** Here we go! They generally have life in hand but are often facing family pressures and money problems. They have competence and some experience and are developing confidence and respect both for and from their peers.

- **The 50s.** Time to produce! At this age, professionals have mastered many of the tools and have earned the boss and peer confidence needed to successfully execute missions and create new paths. On the personal side, it may be crunch time as a result of years of less-than-ideal habits around diet, exercise, and other behaviors (often related to the manner in which they shed stress).

- **The 60s.** At this stage, people are maximizing production and creating "coattails" for others to hang onto. In other words, they are mentoring others to successful lives and careers even as they themselves are mentored in other areas. Physical issues begin to get in the way. Sometimes (not always!) people at this age are starting to slow down a bit.

- **The 70s.** People in this age group are either enjoying the rewards of a successful life and lifestyle or frustrated with the circumstances in which they find themselves because they sacrificed the future for early immediate gratification. If you find yourself mentoring someone late in life, hopefully your mentee is a member of the first category. For many smart seniors, even as they mentor others, they still seek to learn for personal enrichment and the desire to contribute in new ways. Physical issues can begin to multiply but will not dampen the spirit of the thoughtfully aging person who comes to grips with how the life cycle works.

It has been my experience that younger people tend to seek advice on how to achieve and succeed while older folks are frequently looking for solutions to rectify a bad decision (or a series of bad decisions). The exception to this is usually the older person contemplating a job change or a positive lifestyle adjustment.

In the case of the former, the rising high achievers, the conversation is always about opportunity and fulfillment. In the latter case, an adult in recovery mode, the conversation is usually the result of a mistake of commission or omission and is more about salvage and resurrection. For young emerging leaders, I give informational advice; cite examples; and offer good outside books, articles, and audio/video resources. For the older "recovering" mentee, my style is to ask instructive questions rather than give answers. Here, the best approach for me is to work together with the mentee to explore options and possibilities until *they* come up with the best path to the fix.

As Sherry will discuss later, there also can be many age, gender, and cultural challenges in good matching for effective mentoring relationships. It is important to think about all of this when you are selecting your mentee or doing the mentor-mentee matching on a larger scale. Yet I will tell you that a good and dedicated mentor, a good and self-motivated mentee, and the right chemistry between the two can and will overcome almost all challenges.

As I close this chapter, I want to reiterate how important it is for a mentee to possess passion, motivation, and a genuine desire to learn from you, the mentor. This is a quality that can't be faked. When you see it in a mentee, you can safely bet that this person will go on to do great things in life.

Here is a quote I feel proves my point. Dr. G. Wayne Clough, author, former president of the Georgia Institute of Technology, and former secretary of the Smithsonian Institution, had this to say:

> One of the smartest things I ever did as a young person was to take the time to identify people I wanted to work with and in that way get them to mentor me. They were people (old gorillas in your terminology) who were smart, polished, good communicators, and had excellent judgment about situations and people. I would go into their office and say, "I would like to work

with you. I know I don't know all I should, but I am a fast learner, and you will never regret taking me on." It always worked.

If you can find a mentee with this attitude, know that you've been given a wonderful gift!

CHAPTER 3

One-on-One, Across the Table

Should you wait for an invitation to the mentoring party? Absolutely not! Be alert for mentoring opportunities with obvious talent. Seize the day! You don't have to wait to be asked…

Once, during my Waffle House career, a talented young restaurant manager asked me, "When is someone going to start developing me?"

I told him, "We're going to begin right now. I'd like a copy of it later, but for the time being, please give me an idea of your self-development plan."

He looked at me with that "deer-in-the-headlights" blank stare.

I said, "You don't have a self-development plan, do you?"

He answered, "No, sir, I don't."

I asked him how he could expect others to invest time in his development if he was not willing to do so himself. I told him, "No one knows your strengths and weaknesses better than you do. If you are honest with yourself, you have the best chance of maximizing your strengths and shoring up your weaknesses."

My new mentee and I then worked together to build his own personal self-development plan. This exercise is critical to anyone's personal improvement for two reasons. First, the act of creating a list of strengths and weaknesses is self-revealing and creates a sense of great self-awareness. Beyond that, the plan is a necessary tool for daily improvement in the life of a seriously engaged mentee.

I was careful to not allow this young man to cheat on the "weaknesses" portion of his plan by saying things like, "I try too hard," or, "I'm too nice to other people." Obviously, these are not real weaknesses. They are self-serving softballs that are thrown out when the mentee does not want to look deep for areas that really need improvement.

By the way, this was the first of many, many conversations I had with this young man throughout his Waffle House career. He listened, worked hard, and went on to become a senior player in Waffle House operations.

The importance of a self-development plan is not necessarily intuitive. Sometimes even a rising star with great potential requires an introduction to that need and a push in that direction.

A Powerful Starting Point for Self-Improvement (an Assignment for the Mentee)

I like lists and exercises. I think they help organize the content of a person's life and help set a positive direction. There are three exercises I find tremendously useful in helping a mentee to sort things out and identify the right paths to take. First would be a candid look at the mentee's strengths and weaknesses. Second is a solid plan for self-improvement. Finally, a "personal reality check" helps identify what the mentee feels is really important in his or her life.

The first exercise is where it all starts: a candid, straightforward evaluation of what the mentee is good at and what he or she is not so good at. This is where they "get real" about their strengths and weaknesses. This is the mentee's inventory of abilities and proficiencies that are there to be maximized and also the shortcomings, flaws, and deficits that need to be shored up.

I think a great way to encourage your mentee to get started with this honest self-evaluation of strengths and weaknesses is to follow a dialog that sounds like this:

"The first step to self-improvement and personal success is coming to grips with what we are good at and what we need to work on. Here is a really good way for you to do that. First, sit down by yourself in a quiet space with pen and paper. Draw a line down the middle of the paper. Label the left and right sides of the line (appropriately), STRENGTHS and WEAKNESSES. Then just let your thoughts flow on to the paper, what you believe you are good at and where you feel the need for improvement or where you could use some help.

"Now, put the paper in the drawer overnight and look at it the next day. New thoughts and ideas will come to mind, and you can add them to the list. An honest list of strengths and weaknesses is best done in a few sittings, eventually involving the input of people you trust to be frank with you.

"If you have a trusted friend or colleague who will be candid with you, discuss with them the list you have developed and request their opinion about the accuracy of your personal assessment. Then ask for honest insights on what you should add to either side of the list. Absolute honesty and candor is critical here, because this list drives the second important exercise: your self-development plan."

Next, it's important for you, as the mentor, to point out that once a person has developed a solid evaluation of their "assets and liabilities"—that is, what they have to offer and what could hold them back—it's time to go to work. Just having the list won't accomplish anything. That person must put together a self-development plan and work hard to acquire the resources and skills to maximize those strengths and shore up the weaknesses. These resources can take many forms, such as books and articles, educational classes, skill-development through personal trial and error, or good advice from respected and more informed or more experienced individuals.

Making progress on even a small self-development list of strengths and (especially) weaknesses can be challenging, even frustrating. So, when I mentor someone regarding their self-development plan, I say, "Don't try to eat the whole elephant at once. Take it one bite at a time. Pick the one strength and one weakness that interest you the most and go to work on them first. Feel good about your progress with those before you act on the others."

Those two exercises can be demanding for the mentee, but what he or she ends up with is a critical guide to self-improvement and success.

The third essential assignment for the mentee is a "personal reality check." This exercise is invaluable for anyone when sorting out options and making high-impact decisions. The "personal reality check" exercise is discussed at length in a future chapter.

There Is No Such Thing as "One-Size-Fits-All" Mentoring

Mentoring is not an "off-the-rack" solution. It's not about sitting across the table with a small black box containing the secret of a successful life, ready to share that same valuable message over and over with every mentee. It's not like a routine assignment given by the Economics 101 college professor who stands in his classroom as each wave of sophomore students rolls through to learn the same thing: the difference between microeconomics and macroeconomics.

Successful mentoring is a carefully tailored approach. The mentor evaluates each mentee based upon their particular merits, determining apparent deficits and successfully filling in the gaps, and matching unique, individual needs with appropriate solutions.

Clearly then, the first step in mentoring is *not* to begin handing out advice and dispensing wisdom! The first job (and greatest challenge) of a good mentor is to size up the mentee. It is to assess what that mentor is working with and to evaluate the mentee in terms of what they say they want versus the reality of what is evident they actually need.

It is equally important to evaluate the apparent current potential of the person with whom you are working. You may think it a bit harsh, but I mentally give my new mentee a numerical 1-10 overall benchmark grade where 5 is the average talent level I see in the college or work environment. This is strictly subjective and not to be shared. It gives me a baseline "reality check" on what I'm working with. Some mentors would rather turn a 4 into a 6 (salvation). Others, including me, are more inclined to make a 10 out of a 6 or 7 (construction). Both pursuits are a noble calling.

Corporate chief officers (CEOs, COOs, CMOs, CIOs, CTOs, et al.) are usually more interested in expanding the talents of higher-capacity individuals and replacing, rather than marginally improving, those who are of lower capacity. If you are starting an executive mentoring program, stay tuned. Sherry will address this topic in more depth later on in this book.

The First Conversation:
Sizing Up the Mentee

The "getting-to-know-you" stage of mentoring is best done face-to-face in a casual setting. Virtual works but not as well as a live conversation where you can get a sense of energy and body language. Over lunch or a cup of coffee, take the time to explore the mentee's wants, needs, and potential. This is the point where you decide if the "fit" is right between the two of you and whether the mentee is best helped by you or someone else.

The more you know about a mentee, the better equipped you are to understand his or her motivation and real needs. Background information helps you understand how the mentee arrived to you at this point in time and what they bring to the party. Their current activities and pastimes help you connect through mutual interests, and the mentee's plans for the future are very telling of his or her self-appraisal regarding reach and grasp.

If your mentee has a high school GED, no interests outside of PlayStation gaming, and thinks the next step is to be the CEO of Microsoft...that tells you something. If they have a highly technical, educational background with few interests outside the IT world and they want to be the world's best code writer, you can waste a lot of time trying to lead them toward that open sales manager's position.

So, through casual conversation and some "icebreaker" questions, it is important to evaluate the mentee's:

- Social skills
- Background/history: family, education, sports, clubs
- Work history
- Technical ability: areas of expertise, certifications, awards
- Civic activity
- Hobbies

- Desires and direction
- Energy and drive (part of the "Eight Great Social Tells" mentioned later)

All that said, here are some good icebreaker questions to ask in the first meeting:

- Where are you from, originally? Where did you grow up?
- Tell me about your family: mom, dad, brothers, and sisters.
- What do/did you like/dislike in high school/college/your last job/this job?
- Do you like what you're doing? What do you absolutely want to achieve/accomplish in the next three years?
- What do you do for fun?
- What are you working on now? What are you trying to get done? What would you really like to do?
- What are you reading? What was the last book you read?
- Do you have a list of written goals?

Sometimes we find ourselves mentoring older, more experienced businesspeople and organizational leaders. In such cases, questions like, "Tell me about your mom and dad and what you liked the most about high school," would, of course, be irrelevant. Here are some bonus questions for the professionals you are mentoring:

- What keeps you awake at night?
- What was your greatest business victory? What didn't go so well (crashed and burned)?
- So, the phone rings during off hours and you know someone has a problem. Before you answer it, who is the face you see in your mind at the other end of the line? (Note: That's the person they need to either retrain or reassign.)
- What are your company's top priorities and do they mesh or conflict with yours?
- If you were president/CEO, what would you do?
- If you are the organizational leader, what is your vision of the future and your strategy to get there?

As you go deeper into the relationship with any mentee (young or experienced), you should become very aware of:

- What's their full background (including parents and siblings)?
- What's important to him or her?
- What makes them happy/sad/afraid?
- Are they aware of their own strengths and weaknesses? If not, start here.
- Do they have a personal self-development plan like the one previously discussed? If not, prompt the exercise and follow up.
- Do they have goals? Are they written? Be sure to discuss.
- What are the issues/problems/challenges currently confronting the mentee?
- What does the mentee really want and want to do?
- What is their vision of themselves five years from now? Ask…Who do you want to be? Why? Where? Doing what? What is your definition of a successful career and life for you?

Having a good grasp on the answers to all of these questions will help you really get to know the mentee as a person. This, in time, will help you personalize the plan the two of you create together. Plus, the more you know about the mentee, the more authentic, productive, and rewarding your relationship will be.

Where to Begin the Mentoring Process

After the initial conversation, you should have developed enough information to be able to assess your mentee's current status and upside potential. (Understand that it will be just an initial estimate. You can be surprised—pleasantly or unpleasantly—later.) To be sure you get all the information, your initial assessment should consider a combination of displayed social skills, intellect, drive, and technical ability. I call this package the "Eight Great

Social Tells," the behavior that drives your first impression of the mentee and his or her potential.

Appraising the Eight Great Social Tells

In any serious business or social arena, personal characteristics that distract from the individual's bearing and carriage are a liability. It may be that you will have to start with social development before or in concert with advice on business and technical issues based on your knowledge in the area of your mentee's personal interests.

There are eight characteristics we immediately notice about another person on first contact, whether in a job interview, at a party, or in any other social context. The impressions in these eight areas give the perceptive observer clear information about where this person has been, how well they are doing, and where they are most likely headed in their career and life. Even if we are not consciously appraising the other person, we still unconsciously notice these things, particularly if they stand out in a positive or negative way.

If your antenna goes up on any of the following, you now have a new place to start on the mentoring journey:

1. Attitude: If not the first thing observed, this is definitely the most important.

2. Energy: We're talking here about energy level in the conversation. What is the mentee's voice level? Inflection? Projection?

3. Appearance: Dress/hair/personal hygiene. Does the mentee look and dress the part?

4. Command of the Language: Vocabulary/use of appropriate words.

5. Engagement: Ability to engage and be engaging. Is the mentee following your conversation with eye contact? Does their conversation hold your interest and do they have an engaging smile?

6. Conversational Bearing: Where are they in the conversation? Lagging, tracking, or leading?

7. Demeanor: Is the person calm and thoughtful or frenetic and over the top?

8. Body Language: How is the person's posture? Eye contact? Does he or she lean forward or backward?

Each of these "tells" deserves a closer look, because it is likely you will be coaching with respect to one or more of them. Let's examine each one:

Attitude

Your attitude is the single most-observed thing about you. People notice it more than your fancy car, more than your flashy clothes, more even than your amazing good looks. Long after they forget everything else about you, they'll remember whether you had a terrific attitude or a terrible one. People with great attitudes are a magnet for great experiences. People with poor attitudes are magnets for bad experiences (which they usually blame on you, me, or bad luck).

Even if a person's attitude is not the first thing noticed, it is the thing most remembered about him or her and the last thing forgotten. Attitude is absolutely the most impactful of the observed characteristics. A great attitude trumps any deficits in other areas and makes us want to reach out and help. A bad attitude leaves us cold. It makes us want to distance ourselves from the unhappiness and the probable bad consequences to follow. I can't think of a single example of anyone improving his or her situation by displaying a bad attitude. Can you?

Here is a good thing to share with someone starting or changing jobs:

"Think about this. When you, as a new employee, show up for the first day at work, you bring no real immediate value to the party in the way of company benefit. As a matter of fact, you are a drain as the company dedicates valuable resources to the necessary functions of onboarding and training you.

"So, on your first day, all you really bring and have to offer is attitude. That means it had better be a great one!"

If your mentee has a bad (or mediocre) attitude, this is where you must start and where you have to stay until you (or professional help) can figure it out and put him or her back on the right track. With a great attitude, almost anything is possible. With a bad attitude, nothing else matters.

Attitude Prevails:
The Judy Thomas Blanton Story

The name "Judy Thomas Blanton" is iconic in Waffle House lore. That Judy became one of the most successful franchisees in Waffle House history takes second place to the fact that she has absolutely the brightest outlook and most positive attitude on the planet.

Judy started her Waffle House career in our training department working with company managers, hourly associates, and also with some of our franchisees who needed a little extra help. After a couple of years in the training role, Judy decided she wanted to get into restaurant operations and eventually start her own franchise. At the time, I thought this to be very dangerous for her. It's a known fact that the financial cemeteries are full of people with little or no restaurant operations experience who thought it would be "fun" to open a restaurant. And remember, high-achieving Judy had a multi-unit franchise in mind.

Yet Judy was undaunted by my concerns. Her unsinkable spirit and her never-say-never, "can-do" attitude convinced Waffle House CEO Joe Rogers Jr. to give her a try as an independent franchisee. Joe gave Judy a "let's-see-what-you-can-do" three-unit operation in Dayton, Ohio. Sadly, at that time, these three restaurants held the unpleasant distinction of being some of the lowest sales-volume Waffle Houses in the nation.

Judy met the challenge head-on. She went to work setting high standards and hiring people who also displayed her wonderful attitude and outlook. She led with energy and charisma. She made friends with customers, associates, and vendors, alike. Her wonderfully infectious attitude inspired everyone with whom she came into contact. Everyone who met Judy admired her and wanted to see her succeed.

Judy did more than succeed. She developed those three marginal restaurants into some of the highest sales-volume units in the Waffle House system. She went on to build a super-successful 35-restaurant, multi-city franchise and broke all sales records to become the highest sales-volume-per-restaurant franchisee in Waffle House history.

Starting with little operational experience, Judy built every bit of that tremendous success on a foundation of high standards and the best attitude I've ever seen.

Energy

More specifically, I'm talking about the energy level and enthusiasm displayed in the mentee's conversation. Relationship-wise, people are either a "sink" or a "source." Some folks are super-exciting to be around. The enthusiasm they have is contagious and waiting to be shared with others as they become a source of energy simply by their presence. At the other end of the spectrum is the "drain"—the person whose energy level is so low you can almost feel them depleting yours.

The space between the two extremes is where most folks live, and that's not a bad thing. The problem is that a middling, uninspired energy level usually produces ordinary experiences and mediocre results. Not good, not bad, just adequate.

In one of my most wonderful experiences as a mentor, I had the pleasure of counselling a young professional woman named Olevia McNally. She had it all. She was brilliant, beautiful, driven, and totally engaged in her business and life. What she didn't display strongly was the strength of her convictions and a confident voice to deliver them to the world. She spoke ever so softly, and you could almost feel her listening to herself talk in order to ensure she was saying everything correctly.

Today she is a very, very successful executive in her company, a director on several boards, and president of at least two large civic organizations. She has received so many awards for her leadership in both the business and community spaces that *Bella* magazine published a feature article on her achievements. What happened?

With so much going for Olevia, I had only two pieces of advice that we focused on every time we met:

1. "Imagine that when you walk into a room, that room ignites! It lights up simply by and because of your presence. You become the source of energy in the room." She initially told me she didn't think she could do that because she would come across as brash, overbearing, and phony. I told her, "Not possible." That kind of exaggerated behavior was simply not in her DNA. Ironically, with other people on similar occasions, I had advised them to "lighten up." But, for this young lady and from where she was starting, "ignite the room" was appropriate advice.

2. "When you are talking with someone, consciously raise your voice level ten decibels." Project!!! Speak not just to the

person but slightly "through" the person and "paint" your conversation on them! Look them in the eye and make them feel what you feel.

It must have worked. Olevia is a superstar.

By the way: Even if someone is an introvert by nature, they can still have a strong energetic presence. As I told the young lady we just discussed, it's not about being loud or bold or inauthentic. It's more about confidence and intention—about being "real" and fully present in the room.

Appearance

"You never get a second chance to make a great first impression."

—Will Rogers

Dress, hair, and personal hygiene say a lot about a person's self-image. But if you are going to be critical, you must consider the person's personal circumstances. Don't expect a college sophomore to show up in a business suit. Do expect a businessperson seeking leadership advice to show up dressed like a leader.

You have to cut people a little slack in this area. I always try to think about what the rest of their closet looks like and why they chose this option. College kids wear jeans and tend to have longer, less fashioned hair. Businesspeople wear slacks and dresses, and the hair is usually more polished and professional-looking.

That said, I am as thrown off by someone who overdresses as I am by someone who underdresses. I'm talking about the person who shows up for a casual meeting in a suit and a silk shirt with French cuffs, cufflinks, and a perfectly knotted silk tie. All you are looking for here is "dress appropriately for the moment" and an appearance that says, "I respect and take care of myself."

Command of the Language

How someone expresses themselves verbally says a great deal about their education and their circle of friends, who probably speak in a similar fashion. Poor grammar is always a great distraction in any conversation and a detriment to effective communication. However, a little grace is due here for the folks with English as a second language.

One-on-one, there are three types of verbal expression that will come at you from across the table: over-speak, under-speak, and on point.

Over-speak. Sometimes words can get in the way of a conversation. The use of a paragraph when a sentence will do can be distracting. "I know you believe you understand what you think I said but I'm not sure you realize that what you heard is not exactly what I meant" is better said, "You heard correctly but I misspoke." I am equally amused by the folks who use big, multi-syllable words where small words will do. Nothing is more transparent than the incorrect use of what my wife calls "Neiman Marcus words" spoken hopefully to impress the listener. When someone says, "I have disdain for the sanctimoniously insincere service of behemoth colloquy," instead of, "I don't like it when people use large, inappropriate words," look out!

This kind of rhetoric (now I'm doing it!) may come from a confidence problem born of the feeling that the person is in "over his head" and needs to measure up. In any event, over-speak hurts a person's authenticity. If an "over-speaking" mentee has potential, your first job may be to raise their self-confidence.

Under-speak. There are several kinds of under-speak. Some of the most common examples are the use of casual language in a more formal setting, using slang in a substantial conversation, and the use of profanity any time. When I talk with college kids, I hear a lot of colloquialisms—"It was amazing, Mr. Thornton. It was like…wow!"

That works well on the campus but not so well in the boardroom or at a job interview. The frequent use of slang like, "I ain't gonna do it," or, "Yo, man. OMG. He's a very cool dude!" is telling. It shows either a lack of education or laziness and possibly a below-average social environment. Profanity (I won't give any examples here!) is the most distracting form of under-speak. It is usually used to exclaim a point, impress the listener, or fill up space when the speaker has run out of legitimate words. Profanity is always inappropriate in any conversation, whether formal or casual.

On point. Someone has command of the language when he or she speaks in a concise manner, using words and phrases appropriate to the subject matter and the conversation. I am impressed when people display the confidence of an understanding of their words and the ability to use them to completely and accurately express their point of view.

Engagement

This is not the "ring on the finger" kind of engagement. It refers to a person who displays talent at creating interest through delivery and shows the capacity to stay on track in the conversational "give and take." There is a great deal of power in the ability to make someone comfortable in front of you, and the truly great communicators all have this ability. People who are comfortable in their own skin show it by being attentive to your conversation (engaged) and by entreating you to be attentive to theirs (engaging). The secret weapon is the knowledge that nothing is more disarming than a sincere, friendly smile.

Conversational Bearing

In the business space, we all have worked with or led three types of colleagues and subordinates:

- "Drag-along Charlie": The guy who always lags behind and never catches up

- Those folks who keep the pace and work right along beside you
- That exceptional person who makes you hustle in order to stay out ahead of them (a wonderful gift)

The same three types often reveal themselves in how they approach conversation:

- If you have to do all the talking, initiate all the conversation, and drag the other person along every step of the way, it tires you out. It's frustrating.
- If you are comfortable in the conversation, your counterpart probably is as well. Someone with a good conversational bearing shares equally in the "give-and-take" exchange of thoughts and ideas.
- If you are lucky enough to be in the presence of a mentee who takes charge of the conversation at appropriate times and makes you raise your game a bit, know that this person has a great future. What's more, working with him or her will be an incredibly rewarding experience.

Demeanor

This is an issue of style and personality. The calm and thoughtful person is easy to deal with—so easy that you may not even notice the casual way in which they comport themselves. Conversely, it is uncomfortable and distracting to sit across the table from someone who is a non-stop talker or has a frenetic, "over-the-top" personality. Faced with that kind of unpredictable demeanor, I spend most of my time wondering what is going to happen next.

Body Language

There have been many books written about body language and seminars held to help us understand it. If you are unfamiliar, I urge you to do some study on this fascinating topic. Most of us, however, know the basics:

- Leaning forward = the person is engaged
- Head tilted = the person is *really* engaged
- Leaning back = they might not be engaged
- Leaning back with legs crossed and arms folded across the chest = disagreement and definitely *not* engaged. You've lost them.
- Hands interlocked in front of them or in the "steeple position" (looks like praying hands) = this person has confidence

Basic body language is not that complicated. I simply observe posture and, most importantly, eye contact. The presence of both means to me self-confidence and comfort in the environment. The absence of one or both means the opposite.

You might consider becoming more aware of your own body language. According to Thai Nguyen, editor of *The Utopian Life*, awareness of your body language, posture, and mannerisms improves your confidence and self-esteem. Even though painful, try watching a video of yourself and see if some personal adjustments are in order.

When We Evaluate, We Don't Notice the Norm

One more thought about observation and what we consciously notice: There is so much stimuli coming at us 24/7 that we tend to filter out what we expect to see and hear. Our social antenna seems to be geared toward things outside the "norm." That means we notice things that exceed our expectations or fall dramatically short. No one gets up in the morning and thinks to himself, *Gee, my teeth feel great again today.* We accept the expected without thought or comment and "pick up on" the unexpected, something way above or way below average for the circumstances.

An observant mentor will use all these "social tells" to evaluate the mentee, to determine if one or more of these social characteristics is necessarily the place to start the mentoring process, and, if so, how much work it will take.

What's Next?

Based on your assessment, you should then decide where to start the mentoring process and create a plan. You must choose where to take the best first steps in adding value to this person's life. What if, in the initial conversation, you learn the mentee wants to be a rocket scientist but in your deep dive you discover mediocre grades in math and physics? What if he or she expresses a desire to be a sales manager, but you see a shy, quiet person sitting before you? What if the mentee would like to pursue a career as a financial advisor with Morgan Stanley and has the smarts but shows up for your first meeting in a wrinkled shirt and with an unkempt haircut?

Here's the point: It's important to *begin where the need is*. I call this starting point the "Learn List" of things that must be taught immediately and the subsequent skills the mentee should learn over time. Almost certainly, you will be initially moving forward on one or more of six fronts:

1. Deportment and Projection: This, of course, connects to the Eight Great Social Tells we just discussed. It also includes the person's mastery of the soft skills Sherry discusses in Step 3 of her Seven-Step Process. See page 137.

2. Education: You might end up recommending certain books, articles, classes, and so forth.

3. Inspiration: Sometimes that's what they really need.

4. Motivation: Again, sometimes that's all they need. (NOTE: You may think inspiration and motivation are the same thing, but they really aren't. Keep reading in this chapter to learn more!)

5. Technical Knowledge: This is the "how-to" part you know so well.

6. Contacts/Networking: Here we're talking about brokering relationships.

Learn List Item 1: Deportment and Projection

Your initial assessment of the mentee's positive or negative social skills is important, because it's the same impression others will have in the business space or society in general. If the mentee comes across as a low-energy person who does not communicate well, this has to be fixed before you can move on. For that matter, if your antenna goes up on any of the Eight Great Social Tells, you now have a new place to start.

For the mentee who checks all the social skills boxes on the plus or neutral side, we have the luxury of moving on from Deportment and Projection to Education, Inspiration, Motivation, Technical Knowledge, and Contacts/Networking.

Learn List Item 2: Education

As a successful businessperson, you have read and continue to read a number of books on a wide range of topics. Many of these books that were so beneficial for you can be equally valuable to the education and enlightenment of others. Hopefully, you have already developed your reading list of the most valuable and impactful books, articles, audio and video resources, podcasts, streaming videos, and online learning websites you have encountered in your own personal growth. Having handy this written list of your top references will be indispensable as you offer educational advice to your mentee.

If you are working with a technically or academically oriented mentee, be prepared to answer questions about future educational needs, certification requirements, and the like.

Learn List Item 3: Inspiration

Occasionally you will encounter a mentee who has all the right stuff but just needs a little spark or a little nudge—a little inspiration or a lot of motivation. The difference between inspiration and motivation is the difference between, "What if you…?" and, "I think you should…!"

For a mentee who has the energy and drive but lacks the right idea or the correct approach to an issue, I find instructive questions are better than answers. Questions like, "Have you thought about…?" and, "What would happen if…?" challenge and inspire. One of my favorite questions is, "We know what we're thinking about. What are we not thinking about?" All provide a path, a channel. Instructive questions spark the mentee's existing energy in a productive direction.

Often, a mentee will be strong in many areas but surprisingly weak in one. Successful, highly productive people have flaws just like everyone else. In the broad spectrum of things, these flaws are usually not very wide but they can run deep. Many times they're so deep that the person is blind to the flaw. A subtle trick to "inspire" in this case is to encourage the mentee to research the issue about which they are uninformed or to practice the exercise they are incapable of performing and master it so well they can *teach it to others*, starting with you. The trick here is that in order to teach, we first must learn—and when we find we have to teach something, we dive in and learn it well.

We Learn Best by Teaching

When I was a Dallas, Texas, Waffle House division manager, I had a very talented district manager named Harlan Simmons. Harlan did everything right except for one thing: He couldn't keep his restaurants clean to my standards. They were what we call "customer acceptable" but just not acceptable to me. I knew he could do better.

I got the idea to ask Harlan to teach a class at our next all-management meeting on "How to Clean a Waffle House So It Shines." We always held these meetings each Thursday in the back room of one of our Waffle Houses. The restaurant I had selected for the meeting just happened to be his perennial cleanliness offender. Harlan gave a great presentation to his peers in the cleanest Waffle House in the nation on that particular day.

Thereafter, Harlan's restaurants were always the cleanest in our division, and I discovered a secret that I carry to this day: People learn best by teaching.

Learn List Item 4: Motivation

For the mentee who has the right idea or has already decided on the correct path but lacks either the self-confidence or the passion for the first step, a mental kick in the pants may be the best bet. Not everyone is looking for answers. Some folks just need to know it's okay to take the next step, to try the next thing or to move forward on a great idea.

Mentees who have everything they need for achievement but the drive to achieve it are the greatest challenge. The problem could be mental or it could be physical. The solution could be diet, exercise, or more sleep, or it could be that the weight of the social world or family circumstances is sapping constructive energy.

Probing questions can help identify the problem but be careful about offering solutions above your pay grade. In cases involving psychological issues, I always consult professionals, because back in the days when "I knew it all," the pros would tell me I was giving the exact opposite of correct advice. If you have hinted, suggested, and urged to no avail, it may be time to bring in a professional.

Usually though, it's just a matter of pushing back from the mentoring table, physically leading the mentee to the starting line, and getting him or her engaged until momentum develops.

Learn List Item 5: Technical Knowledge

This is where the naïve mentee thinks you will start and believes it is why you are sitting across the table. The act of sharing specific technical knowledge is a very important part of the process, and once all the other boxes are checked, this is where you will excel. If the filter system matching you and the mentee has worked properly, you will be able to impart a great deal of technical, meaningful advice and very pointed information relative to the mentee's area of specific interest.

Learn List Item 6: Contacts/Networking

A key attribute of senior leadership in any business or civic organization is the ability to successfully broker relationships. Sometimes these relationships are internal, pulling departments together in the execution of a large company project, and sometimes these relationships are inter-organizational, forming productive alliances with outside businesses and organizational groups.

A mentor has the same responsibility with his or her mentee. In many cases (and in most cases with superstar mentees), you will want to connect your charge with other business and organizational captains for the benefit of further education, problem-solving, employment, or networking.

Remember that a key component in your mentee's personal success equation is not only who he or she knows but, more importantly, who personally knows your mentee. Critical in that regard is that your mentee ends up in business with the correct person. You know the good ones. Your mentee does not.

Getting Started on the Right Foot

The first one-on-one meetings with a mentee are tremendously important because they form the foundation for a successful mentoring experience. Taking enough time up front so you build a relationship and truly know who your mentee is and where he or she needs the most help is the critical first step. Sure, you will discover more about your mentee as time goes on, but these first meetings will set the stage for your relationship.

It is also possible that, based on these first few conversations and what you learn from them, you or the mentee may decide this is not the right relationship. That's okay. Everyone is not a perfect fit. Just be glad you figured it out early on so both of you can move on to someone who is a better match.

CHAPTER 4

Moving Along in the Relationship

As you move into this chapter, you've presumably had several meetings with your mentee. By now you should have a good feel for who your mentee is in several areas. For example:

- Social skills
- Areas of technical interest
- Real coaching needs
- Real potential

At this point, you are probably working on a few things simultaneously: some deportment (behavior) challenges, some educational opportunities, and perhaps a little motivation and inspiration. If you are sold on the mentee's potential, you may have already pulled out the contact list to see who can help with jobs or additional information.

Regardless of the mentee's specific interest or potential, there are several really good tools to use and approaches to take in order to accelerate their personal and business growth. There are also several teachable, fundamental concepts that are critical to your mentee's success. We will cover them in the next few chapters.

First, consider this list of tools and approaches:

- Schedule regular meeting times with your mentee. Sherry will point out that some degree of flexibility is needed here but structure does count. Suggest a target time to get started (like the first Wednesday of each month), but be prepared to adjust if necessary. Be sure to encourage the mentee to check in between meetings whenever needed.
- Develop the "Learn List" (as presented in Chapter 3) for what your mentee needs to learn immediately and within the next 12 months. Your mentee should get a copy to work from and, of course, you will keep a copy. Note: In the corporate setting, if you are assigning this mentee to another mentor, everybody gets a copy of the Learn List: the mentee, the mentor, and you, so you can check progress.
- Coach rather than deliver solutions. When the answers are obvious to you, there is a great deal of value in not simply providing them. Instead of providing those solutions, teach your mentee how to think through problems. Talk about the importance of considering choices and their consequences, especially the unintended consequences. (Teach your mentee "*how* to fish" versus simply "*giving* him a fish.")
- Read *Find an Old Gorilla: Pathways Through the Jungle of Business and Life* and have your mentee read it. Use it as a "bridge" to discuss relevant growth and leadership topics found throughout this book.
- Develop a reading list based on your favorite articles and books on various topics and recommend them to the mentee. Follow up with questions.
- Create a catalog of friends and colleagues whose strengths and business positions are suited to your mentee's needs. This is the list you will use to help your mentee network

at higher levels by making introductions and brokering re-lationships.

- As a frustrated mentor, don't be afraid to phone a friend for help or hand the mentee off to another (more aligned) resource.
- Expect the meeting structure and content to evolve over time. A rigid agenda gets in the way of a good mentor who is reacting to what he sees and hears. Early on, you (the mentor) are in control and asking most of the questions. Success comes when those probing questions (looking for information about the mentee) turn into instructive ques-tions (provoking constructive answers and solutions from the mentee). Over time, the mentee will begin to come pre-pared, take control, and run the meeting. That's real personal growth.

Of course, this is not a comprehensive list. These are just a few suggestions based on my own experience and preferences. Your background may give you additional, different, and even better tools to use.

Five Critical Fundamental Concepts to Share and Teach or Affirm

There are several key concepts that will greatly influence a rising star's chances for success. You might think these concepts would be understood intuitively, but they are not. Fact is, your mentee may not even be aware of them. It's likely that you learned these realities the hard way, but by emphasizing them early in the rela-tionship, you will give your mentee a big head-start over his or her peers.

If you are mentoring someone in an individual effort, I urge you to weave these concepts into your teachings as appropriate. If you run a large mentoring program, I encourage you to ensure these concepts are unilaterally taught and stressed often. They are:

1. Reward follows performance.

2. Choices have consequences.

3. There are eight personal decisions that can control your destiny.

4. The only thing constant in life is change.

5. If you don't manage your time, everyone else will.

Let's address each one in more detail.

FUNDAMENTAL CONCEPT 1: Reward follows performance.

In the real world, reward follows performance and never precedes it. I like to illustrate that with the story about the man who one day sat in his easy chair in front of the fireplace and said, "Give me some heat and I'll go get you some wood." He wondered why the room stayed so cold. The man did not understand that before you get heat, you must go outside, find the wood, cut it up, drag it back to the house, fill the fireplace and light a fire. If you do it all correctly, *then* you get the heat. Reward follows performance. The proverb "As ye sow, so shall ye reap" has been around for 2,000 years for a good reason…it's true.

We must add value before we can expect to see reward, and that reward seldom comes immediately. My father used to say, "The year knows much the days never see." He meant what you and I know to be true: The scales don't balance every day. It often takes weeks, months, and sometimes years for hard work to pay off. Unfortunately, the average person becomes frustrated when they can't see input and output, cause and effect, or effort and results in the same day. As important as it is to realize that reward follows performance, it is equally important to understand that it rarely follows performance *immediately*. There is no timetable for reward.

Once, a rather unimpressive manager told me he was not going to do something because he was not getting paid for it. I suggested that if he never did any more than he was being paid for, he would never be paid more than he was making right now.

FUNDAMENTAL CONCEPT 2:
Choices have consequences.

There is a difference between what successful people do and what average people do. People who do very well in life don't leave their future to chance. They intentionally make good choices about attitude, appearance, behavior, and direction.

In *Find an Old Gorilla*, we talk about the importance of hanging around the right people. If you want to be successful, choose to spend time with successful people and pay attention to what they do, what they say, and how they act.

We also talk about the importance of honesty in word and deed. Long-term, in business and in life, you cannot be dishonest and survive, let alone thrive. Notice I said, "long-term." There are many people who have enjoyed a brief period of dishonesty and acquired "success" just before they checked into prison. In fact, honesty *is* the best policy, and your long-term success depends on it. As Abraham Lincoln famously said, "No man ever got lost on a straight road."

The truly successful person is honest with friends and business associates alike (in business, with associates both above and below them in the organizational chain). The truly successful person takes personal responsibility for all choices and decisions he or she makes.

Personal Responsibility Payoff

When I was an area vice president in the Southwest, Midwest and far West Waffle House markets, our real estate department had O'Fallon, Missouri, under contract as a potential location. It was a complicated deal. It involved purchase of the property, moving and selling an on-site house for cash, fill work, relocating a fence to avoid an appurtenance, and other issues. My CEO, Joe Rogers Jr., told me to approve the deal if, and only if, our net out-of-pocket dollars were "X" or less.

At crunch time, the real estate director called me from the closing for final approval to sign off on the deal. I told him I had one question: "Does the deal net out to 'X' or less?" He told me it was complicated but his back-of-the-envelope math on the pluses and minuses said yes. I told him to buy.

Unfortunately, that deal came in at a net cost of "X" plus $15,000—not over by much, but over. On his next trip into my market, Joe got off the airplane and asked, "Why did you buy O'Fallon?" I felt the fact that the real estate guy's math was faulty was irrelevant. I was the AVP, and the final decision was mine. My answer was, "Joe, I made a mistake."

His response was that "I made a mistake" was the correct answer. He went on to say there would have been consequences if I had overridden his decision and decided on my own that the property was worth the "add-on" or if I had thought a $15,000 overage was small and acceptable. Seeing I understood, we moved on immediately to other operational topics, and years later he made me president and chief operations officer of Waffle House.

In situations like this, it can be tempting to go straight to blame, rationalization, and victimization. But taking immediate ownership of a problem changes the trajectory of the outcome. If Joe had to convince me that I made a mistake, immediately he would start questioning my judgment. When mistakes are made, you need the energy to fix the problem, and you can't deplete yourself trying to convince people what right looks like. Plus, it damages confidence, trust, and an overall brand when lack of ownership is your first reaction.

Choosing the right direction or "path" is often difficult. Sometimes it is simply an issue of legal versus illegal. Often, we must choose between instant gratification and delayed gratification, meaning a) smooth sailing today and mediocrity tomorrow, or b) sacrifice now and payoff later.

Usually, though, the choices are about how we behave and represent ourselves to others. Most people follow the masses and reduce themselves to the *average*. To excel sometimes means abandoning the "path of least resistance" that most folks travel and deciding to take the more difficult route where traffic is lighter and rewards are (usually) greater.

Unfortunately, most people go through life trying to avoid pain. Successful people are driven by ambition, not the avoidance of pain.

Here is a "cheat sheet" for success. These are the top-ten behaviors (ten and a half, actually) that I routinely see in highly successful people. Besides sharing these with your mentee, you might ask yourself if you are doing any or all of these things.

1. Successful people always take notes. They keep a pen and paper or personal device with them always. They don't try to remember thoughts and facts. They write them down. Moreover, they all seem to keep a file of the best ideas (thought of or heard) and the great articles they have read that seem to resonate the most.

2. They hang around the right people. They associate with people who have things they aspire to have, who do things they aspire to do, and who hold positions they aspire to hold. Successful people hang around these folks and listen. *(Number

2.5 is, while hanging around the right people, they find a mentor who is interested in their success and helps to guide them through the social, political, and cultural aspects of life and business.)

3. They are honest. They know the alternative never works long-term.

4. Successful people keep a great attitude, always. No matter what. This is the most impactful of the "Eight Great Social Tells."

5. They get up earlier than their friends. In the business space, they get up earlier than the competition.

6. They know how and when to say "yes" and how and when to say "no."

7. Successful people are constantly nourishing their minds, their bodies, and their soul/spirit. For example, successful leaders read. If you do not read, you will pay a price for that, over time. Also know there are many books that are not meant to be read only once. They also eat good food and pray or meditate. They are grateful for what they have and lead a life of reciprocation, always ready to give back.

8. A successful person knows how to manage their time. They have goals and take action when other people procrastinate or get bogged down by distractions

9. Successful people give away all the credit and take all the blame. Period.

10. The most successful people I know are philanthropic. They are constantly helping others. They give away things of value and they do it all anonymously. They don't talk about it.

Give It Away...Anonymously

I know a family who, on the first freezing day of every winter, calls all the elementary schools in the community and asks one question: "Who are the children who came to school today with no coats?" Think about it. If it is 32 degrees outside and a child comes to school with no coat, there is only one reason: The child doesn't have a coat.

So, this family gets these children's genders and sizes. They go to stores like Walmart, Old Navy, and Burlington, and they buy some warm jackets. They take them home and pin a child's information in each jacket. They put these coats into black plastic lawn bags, and the next day they take them to the school. Without giving their names, the family leaves the coats at the front desk and asks that they be given to the principal. Then they leave.

Knowing what they've done for those children and not seeking credit for their kindness—keeping the secret of this gift in their hearts—can you imagine what kind of positive power follows them all that day? And, if these anonymous acts of selfless kindness are frequent, can you imagine the positive power their giving brings to their lives?

FUNDAMENTAL CONCEPT 3: There are eight personal decisions that can control your destiny.

A *successful* life is about making good decisions. Being human, we won't make them all correctly, but if we are thoughtful in our choices, we will get most of them right, especially the really big ones that count heavily. In my book *Find an Old Gorilla*, I discuss the eight most impactful personal decisions that ultimately control where you (and your children) end up in life. The choices to be made regarding those decisions are so important that I believe they are worth repeating here.

Whether mentee or mentor, treat these eight life-directing decisions with greater respect and you will enjoy better long-term consequences:

1. **What you (or your children) do in high school, and most importantly, after each school day is finished.** (Structure counts at this age.) Do you play sports, participate in band or drama, or join clubs? Or, do you hang out at the mall with friends? If you do just hang out with friends, at least hang out with friends with ambition. This is where we get in the habit of enriching and challenging ourselves—or not.

2. **If and where you go to college or trade school.** A four-year college degree certainly is not an imperative, but successfully productive people do need some type of post-high-school training. And it's not just about what you study. It's also about the contacts you make that will serve you later in life, often as future business relationships.

3. **Where you go to work.** The field you're in and the company you choose really matter. Essential industries and growing companies set a much better stage for the future.

4. **If and who you marry.** Is your partner your social equal? Does your partner have people skills? Share your ambition? Balance your strengths and weaknesses? Lifetime relationships are built upon mutual respect, shared interests, and teamwork in achievement.

5. **Where you live.** The city, state, and neighborhood you live in will impact your future, not only regarding who you meet and the opportunities that present themselves, but also how your children grow up. It bears mentioning here that as virtual work becomes more and more common, people have a lot more leeway in choosing where they live. It's not always necessary to work in the same city where your company is located.

6. **Children or no children.** It's just a decision and neither is "better" than the other. You have more time early on (and quite possibly more money in the long run) if you choose no kids. But being child-free also means no grandchildren and no continuing family. There are benefits and drawbacks to every decision.

7. **Whether or not you save money.** How do you handle your finances in general? Do you have a plan? A budget? Or do you wing it?

8. **How you relate to the world spiritually.** Do you do so through organized religion? Personal spirituality? Or none?

Each of these decisions will send you (and/or your children) down a very specific path. Think about them all very carefully.

FUNDAMENTAL CONCEPT 4: The only thing constant in life is change.

Change is all around us. As a matter of fact, it's about the only surety in life you can count on. Change will occur…by you, to you, and around you.

My friend Quint Studer is fond of saying, "We need to change the way we think about change." Quint is absolutely correct, and the first step in that process is to simply start thinking about the concept of change—what it is and how it works. The more you understand something the better equipped you are to deal with it. Since your mentee will spend a lifetime wrestling with change, it's a good concept for you to explore with him or her.

There are two kinds of change: initiated and inherited.

Initiated change is the change you start and you control, whether in business or in your personal life. There are always seven steps to initiated change:

1. Denial that a change needs to be made. (Interestingly, the largest state in the nation is not Texas, Alaska, or California. It's the state of Denial. Everyone lives in it at one time or another.)

2. Realization and acceptance that a change needs to be made.

3. Attempt to make the change.

4. Failure to make the change. (We all go through it.)

5. Frustration upon returning to the previous behavior or procedure and either wanting or expecting a different result. (It has been said that doing the same thing and expecting a different result is the height of insanity.)

6. Refocus, reengage, reattempt.

7. Successful change. You can always get to #7, successful change, if you don't get hung up on #4. Now that you know failure is out there and it's a normal part of the process, you can deal with it successfully.

Inherited change is the change you did not start and do not control. It could be in the workplace or in your personal space, but inherited change is all around you and is a part of life. You may like the change or you may not like it, but you definitely do have to deal with it in some way.

It has been said that in the face of inherited change, we can respond in only one of four ways:

1. Mope
2. Hope
3. Dope
4. Cope

Mope: You can always throw a pity party and wring your hands, but the "woe-is-me" attitude won't fix anything and will simply alienate everyone around you (except the other pitiful people who aren't getting anywhere, either).

Hope: You can hope it will get better, change back, go away, etc., but hope alone is not enough. Prayer works but it works best when we work hard, right alongside it.

Dope: You can "dope" about it, stick your head in the sand, and pretend it's not there. (We call this "ostrich management.")

Cope: You can deal with it. The first step in coping with inherited change you don't care for is to honestly ask yourself, *Is this change actually hurting me or am I just annoyed by it?* There is a big difference between pain and discomfort. There is a big difference between inconvenience and injury. It's important to know how you are really being affected because this will influence your coping strategy.

Some people think running away from inherited change you don't like is the same as coping. The reality is that a quick decision to escape may actually bring about a much bigger adverse change. Be very careful with life's four most stressful change events: #1 loss of a loved one, #2 changing relationships, #3 changing jobs, #4 changing residences. It's never a good idea to tackle more than one of these four life changes in the same year.

In the business space, a good CEO or mentor will stress the reality that while the grass always looks greener on the other side of the fence, everyone's grass has dirt on the bottom. You just have to be close enough to see it. This is something to think about before you jump the fence.

Another fact to consider when contemplating a job change (and this one is counter-intuitive) is that change saps momentum. It takes a year or so to assimilate and be assimilated into a new corporate culture. How much ground could have been gained at the former job in that amount of time?

FUNDAMENTAL CONCEPT 5: If you don't manage your time, everyone else will.

We all get the same amount of time: 24 hours in a day, seven days a week, 365 days a year. Successful people don't get more time; they have just learned how to effectively manage the time they are given.

Here is a good way to present the three skills your mentee must learn and apply in order to effectively manage his or her time:

1. **Know where you want to go...** This is called goal-setting, and these goals must be physically recorded somewhere (on a piece of paper or a personal device) so you can look at them every day and routinely evaluate your progress. Goals are the achievements and assets you chase in life and business. Goals focus you, ground you, and define your purpose in life. Zig Ziglar, in his many video presentations, accurately points out that without goals, you are a "wandering generality." He says that goals turn you into a "meaningful specific." If you want to accomplish or attain something, make it a goal. You cannot achieve goals you have not set.

    Note: It is important to understand that your mentee may not really know how to set goals. You may need to have a fundamental discussion about how to determine what is really important, what he or she really wants in life or business, and how to organize personal thoughts and actions around the achievement of those things.

2. **...Then develop an action plan.** Once you know where you want to go, remember that nothing happens until there is an action plan in the execution phase. A good action plan considers what resources are needed, how to manage them, and how to measure the progress through constant follow-up. Consider your goals, marshal your resources, and set deadlines for

yourself and others. Instructions without deadlines are simply suggestions. Written instructions with deadlines that create a sense of urgency will keep action plans on track through a successful finish.

3. **Learn to avoid distractions.** There are hundreds of distractions in life every day. So many young people (and, frankly, older ones too) are addicted to screens/social media today, and it certainly seems to affect their ability to be proactive, effective, and efficient. The challenge is to press through these and other distractions and stay on course.

As an example, I like to share the Biblical story of the seed sower who is casting his seeds one morning when he notices a few birds several rows back pecking at some of the seeds on the ground. At that moment in his life, the seed sower has one very important decision to make: Does he want to be a seed sower or a bird chaser? As it turns out, the seed sower is smart. He knows some of the seeds he casts will find barren ground and will not grow. He knows the wind will blow some seeds up onto rocks, and a few will be eaten by the birds. He also knows that 100 percent of the seeds left in that sack at the end of the day will not grow. So, he avoids the distraction of the birds and continues to sow the seeds that grow the crops his village needs for survival.

Better to be a seed sower than a bird chaser. Better to set the course and avoid distractions. You cannot major in minor affairs in life or business and hope to be successful.

These three tips aren't just for business. They are incredibly valuable for your personal life as well. As an emerging leader in the Waffle House system, I faced the same problem that confronts rising high achievers everywhere: There aren't enough hours in the day or days in the week. My wife, Kathy, was patient (as she always has been), but my five-year-old daughter was getting pushed aside by an ever-growing schedule of business responsibilities. I decided that this work/family life-balance issue had more to do with me than with my business, so I took out my calendar and wrote my daughter Aspen's name on the first open date two weeks away.

Seeing this, Kathy chided me, asking, "Why do you have to write your daughter's name on the calendar to spend time with her?" I answered I had come to a decision. If I simply gave her the time that was "left over," she would never get enough, and that was unacceptable. If I didn't treat her time like all the important events and get it on the calendar, things would "come up" and steal that time, just as it had in the past. Aspen and I had a great day together.

This started a tradition of planned "daddy-little girl dates" with all three of my daughters (Aspen, Chaice, and Mayson) that exists to this day, even though they are all mothers and very successful businesswomen. Now, they put me on their calendars, too!

A footnote here is that when Kathy saw the success of my plan, we created a Monday night, turn-off-the-phones "date night." Just us…and that was a game changer!

CHAPTER 5

Mentoring Aspiring Leaders and Managers

While most people are happy being followers, those who want to plan and execute will grow to become leaders or managers. Some will even strive to become senior leaders and managers willing to, and capable of, taking on a tremendous amount of responsibility.

In this chapter, our conversation will center on coaching your mentee to be a serious producer who gets things done as an effective leader or manager. While everything we said in Chapter 4 applies to these candidates, the advice in this chapter is tailored specifically to those who are mentoring emerging leaders. We'll cover topics ranging from the leadership basics to goal-setting and planning to time management to leading others…and more.

Let's begin with the basics…

Understanding the Basic Leadership Skills Requisite to Success

Peter Drucker, the father of modern management, is thought to have said, "You can't manage what you don't measure." I would add to that the obvious follow-up: "You also can't manage what you don't understand."

Successful leaders and managers think differently from followers. They have an understanding of the special skills required of them in order to effectively lead, and the application of those skills is what sets them apart.

A successful leader must be competent at four things:

1. Understanding concepts and ideas

2. Understanding, managing, and developing people

3. Understanding financial matters, both business and personal

4. Understanding self-discipline, self-respect, self-confidence, and self-image

Understanding concepts and ideas takes a discipline of thought and focus. Understanding, managing, and developing people requires an ability to relate to others and a personal commitment to their success. Financial acumen is simply a skill acquired through education. The big one—the understanding of one's self—is the product of courage. It requires a willingness to look in the mirror and grow.

If your mentee is to excel in the areas of team leadership and project management, he or she must understand these four basics and be able to develop them into personal strengths. For some mentees, the basics are intuitive. For others, they will need to be learned and absorbed. Either is fine as long as you make sure, in the end, they are acquired.

In addition to understanding the first four basics, a successful leader is the voice of reason in conflict. He or she exhibits depth of thought, strong core values, and moral fiber, and is willing to take full responsibility for all of life and business. He or she dresses, acts, and talks like a professional.

The successful leader is also very adept at brokering relationships, both internally (between people within the entity he or she leads) and externally (between that entity and the organizations and leaders with which it makes contact).

Beyond the essential basics, there are additional skills that are important to a leader's efficiency and effectiveness. The more masterful the leader or manager is at these skills, the greater the success in store. In that regard, here is some great advice for you to give the mentee.

Start by Managing Yourself: The Personal Reality Check

This is where the mentee considers the question: *What do you really want, and what do you really want to get done?* We will talk about the importance of developing life and business goals in just a minute. But first, how do you set those goals? How do you know what you really want in terms of assets and achievement?

The personal reality check is a tool to organize your thoughts around your needs, your wants, and the things you really dislike. It's a way to get grounded when you are trying to make decisions in the confusion of life.

On a piece of blank paper, draw two vertical lines dividing the paper into three equal columns. Label the first column "Must Have." Label the second column "Like to Have," and label the third column something like "Will Not Tolerate" or "Cannot Abide."

Now consider your life, your family circumstances, or the decision at hand and start filling in the columns.

In the first column, list all those outcomes that are absolutely essential to your life now and in the future. If considering a specific decision, also include the outcomes that you would absolutely demand happen as a product of that decision.

In the second column, place all the outcomes that would be nice to see, but are not critical. These are bonus items you would like to have but really can do without. These are not deal-breakers.

The third column is a little tricky. It represents outcomes, eventualities, and actions you would not tolerate in your life. For a specific decision at-hand, these are the outcomes you would not abide at the conclusion of the deal you are considering. At a glance, you might think it is the opposite of column one—and sometimes it is. Actually, it is the "I won't go there no matter what" column. The more honest you are about what you place in this column and the more you pay attention to it, the happier and less frustrated you will be.

Once this list is made, you then prioritize your true wants, needs, and desires by numbering them in order of importance. Now go to work on number one.

Here are a couple of "reality check" examples. The first is someone trying to decide what matters most at this time in his or her life. The second is someone considering a job change.

What Is Important to Me in Life

Must Have	Like to Have	Will Not Tolerate
Health	Great-paying job	Bad health habits
Fitness	New car	Job I hate

Loving spouse	Home vs. apartment	People who lie, cheat, and steal
Children	Friendly in-laws	Poor schools for my children
Stable job with room to grow	A leadership role in job/community	
Good friends		
Ample money		
Savings account		
Living expenses covered		

What I Want in a New Job

Must Have	Like to Have	Cannot Abide
At least $90k/year	>$100k/year	Move out of south-east
Good health benefits	Stock purchase opportunity	More stress than now
A leadership role	Company car	Incompetent boss
Growth opportunity	Officership opportunity	
Competent, friendly bosses and associates	Based in Florida	
Job in sales or management	Less stress than now	

Once the mentee has given some thought to what they truly want out of their career and life, they'll be in a position to start setting some goals.

Why Goals Are Critical

Being an effective leader starts with purpose. You have to know where you want to go. We talked some about goal-setting in the previous chapter as it is important for anyone in the workforce who wants to be good at their job. If a mentee wants to be a leader, though, goals are crucial. If you don't know what you want and what you want to get done, you are better off grabbing a Coke and just enjoying the party with the followers.

Many people actually do take that aimless approach to life. They wander around with nothing particular in mind until they feel a stone in their shoe (something that annoys them) and then they have a purpose: to get rid of the stone. But then, once rid of the stone, they wander around some more until another stone finds its way into their shoe.

These folks view life as a defensive game, and they never really play offense. Understand, these may be pleasant people, but they aren't effective and they certainly aren't leaders and managers. If only someone had told them early on how much fun it is to take charge of their lives and had coached them effectively on how to do it!

Purposeful people have goals. Remember that the late Zig Ziglar said that without goals you are a wandering generality, and goals turn you into a meaningful specific. Goals, by the way, are always written down and are not simply carried in your head. Ambitions not written down might be wishes, but they are not goals and are seldom attained.

Goals All Set? Make a Plan and Write It Down

Planning is essential. Think about this: Most people spend more time planning a party than a life. It sounds silly but it's true. Think about some of your friends and the amount of planning they did for their last parties. What if they spent that same amount of time planning their lives?

So, while goals are the first step, you cannot achieve them without taking the second step, which is to put together a good action plan and generate the effort necessary to put that plan into place. When writing down your action plan (yes, writing it down—it can't be just in your head), make sure it answers these critical questions:

- Where specifically is the goal line? What does success look like?
- What needs to happen in order for me to reach my goal?
- What resources do I need?
- Whose help and support do I need?
- What are the obstacles to my achievement?
- What's my timeline? What are the deadlines for achievement at each step?

The leader's job is to create a plan that gathers together the people and resources necessary to get the job done and get it done on time.

Avoid the Trap: Ignore Negative Distractions

Being effective starts with purpose and a good action plan, but it is realized and sustained only with commitment and perseverance. In pursuit of their goals, effective people fully expect to encounter:

- Difficulty
- Resistance
- Setbacks

- Delays
- Naysayers

Knowing these negatives are out there, effective, successful people persist. Even with short-term frustration, they persist. Understanding and expecting these negatives helps lessen the frustration, because they realize it's just a part of the game and they endure and succeed. The negatives will slow down or even stop an unprepared, uninformed, or uncommitted person. Consider the old and true observation, "No matter how stony the path, some forge ahead. No matter how easy the going, some lag behind." Leadership always finds a way.

It is also very important to recognize the difference between "Urgent" and "Important." Some things that appear important are really just urgent. Consider a necessary trip to the bathroom. In the cosmic scheme of things, this is relatively unimportant, but to you and me, it can be very urgent. Sometimes we do need to address the urgent little fires around our feet (or assign them to be addressed by someone else). Yet we should never let them derail the important, mainstream work that is driven by the leader and measured every day. Remember the classic story about the fellow who spent so much time fighting alligators, he forgot his initial objective was to drain the swamp.

The effective manager or leader doesn't fall for the "stone in the shoe" trick. He or she stays focused on the mission and on track with a regular review of the progress…both the positive and the negative aspects. Peter Drucker's rule is so very true. You can't manage what you don't measure.

Focus Your Thoughts and Make the Most of Your Time

We talked a lot about time management in the previous chapter. All of this also applies to emerging leaders, of course. In fact, it's even more important for this group of mentees as their time and attention are in such great demand. Here are some bonus thoughts about time management and personal organization to share with emerging leaders:

- Create and work from a "to-do list." This is a daily work list that can be digital (on a personal device) or analog (pen and paper notes). This tool is essential to working efficiently and effectively toward the achievement of goals.

- Different from the to-do list is the "100-day plan." It's an important but short list of strategic projects or essential tasks to be completed within 100 days. This list is a good tool for staying focused on the pieces that are crucial to the success of the overall strategy. First, write the starting date and also the (self-imposed) deadline date 100 days from today. Next, list the three to five critical-to-the-mission objectives that must and will be achieved by the end date 100 days from today. Review the list every week for progress and adjust accordingly. There is no carry-forward allowed here. Taking something off the list is not an adjustment; it is a cop-out. Unless fortune obviates the need for the goal, you must achieve it, and you must achieve it on time, by the end date.

- Get super-focused with a personal reality check (explained earlier here and found on page 6 of *Find an Old Gorilla*).

- Use a "T" chart for decisions. The idea of a T chart is to list the pros and cons of a particular decision on either side of the stem of a T. If there are more pros than cons, move forward. If not, don't. You can also assign each pro and con a number value based on its importance, and then go with the decision of the column with the highest value.

As a leader, of course, the mentee won't just be managing their own time. They'll be managing the time (and talents) of others. Let's touch on a few high-impact tips for doing it well.

Managing People: Some Basic Rules for Getting Things Done Through Others

Work and achievement are multiplied and accelerated by the effective management of others.

However, managing people can be like herding cats unless you follow a few basic rules:

1. Select your team carefully, based on desire and ability, not seniority and charm.

2. Look beyond seniority and delegate assignments based solely on "want to" and "can do."

3. Make sure you have team "buy-in" on the mission/goal/project.

4. Ensure your team has a full understanding of the goal line and the deadline.

5. Make sure everyone has everything they need (all the tools and resources) required to successfully complete their parts of the project. Don't guess. Ask, "Do you have what you need...?"

6. Compensation can be like the steering wheel on a car. Properly structured, it will guide your team in the direction you choose—toward the accomplishment of their mission and the achievement of your goals. Compensating for a desired outcome will focus someone's attention. People listen to what you say, but they do and pursue what you pay for.

7. Issue clear and specific *written* instructions with deadlines. These instructions are written because they become your team members' goals.

8. Follow up constantly, measuring progress (or lack thereof)

and handing out consequences—good consequences for achievement (whether just a verbal, "Great job!" or an incentive reward) and appropriate consequences for a lack of performance. Negative consequences must reflect the degree and nature of the performance deficit. In some cases, it can be just an, "I believe in you and know you can do better." A renegade who ignores your instruction and blows up a project would get a much more serious measure of censure.

Consequences Don't Have to Be Negative

When I was a young unit manager running Waffle House #66 in Atlanta, I had two salespeople (servers) named Addie and Maybelle working with me as I cooked the morning shift. Both women were excellent servers and even helped me a lot on the grill when it became very busy. (Waffle House later implemented mandatory staffing guidelines of three salespeople every morning and a back-up grill operator as well, in higher-volume situations.)

On one particular morning, I was cooking away when I heard a crash of dishes at the far end of the restaurant at a low-counter area. This was Maybelle's long-standing, everyday station. She had dropped a whole armload of dishes she was clearing from a customer. Maybelle burst into tears and ran to the back room while Addie and I apologized to the customer and cleaned up the mess. I went to the back and asked Maybelle to return to the front to her station. She said she could not. I told her, "Maybelle, there is no one else. You can't let Addie and me down." She replied mysteriously, "I can't wait on him. I just can't do it!

Moments later, Addie came back to tell me Maybelle's customer at the low counter was none other than Merle Haggard (who was later voted the number-one country singer of all time by *Rolling Stone* magazine). Merle liked Maybelle a lot, so whenever he was in town for a concert, he always came to our Waffle House the next morning for breakfast and sat at her station. Maybelle's "consequence" for broken dishes and tears was that when Merle ate with us, Addie and I covered the whole restaurant for the few minutes she spent talking to her favorite country star. Merle was a great guy and ate with us several times while I was the manager of #66.

The obvious note here is that consequences for problematic performance need to reflect some common sense.

Now, let's change direction for a moment. Work, at times, spills over into our personal lives. This is true for everyone, but may be especially true for leaders. The mentee needs to be aware of how to prevent work stress from becoming relationship stress.

Tough Days Will Come; Prepare Yourself and Your Life Partner

Judy T. Blanton (the Waffle House franchisee whom I previously mentioned as having the best attitude on the planet) has crazy days just like the rest of us. She told me once, "Bert, some days you eat the bear, and some days the bear eats you."

When you drag yourself home at the end of "one of those days," a little prior communication with your spouse or partner can help you stay on the right track.

While you might feel great about what's going on right now, it's vital to coach and teach your partner to say the right things when you are "down." Rather than commiserating (sharing in your misery and thus perpetuating it), coach them to listen and help by offering the constructive advice you have pre-programmed with them. (By "pre-programming," I mean talking to them ahead of time about the responses you find helpful.)

For example, we all get stressed out. On that occasion when you come home grumbling about the workload or the "slacker" who can't do his job, ask your partner to be ready to 1) fully hear you out, and 2) ask questions to help you resolve the issue in your head. "Are you delegating everything you can?" "Does the worker understand what you want?" "Is it a capacity problem or perhaps a training problem?"

Sometimes our partners have a natural instinct to want to commiserate or try to comfort us. It's wonderful that they care. Tell them you appreciate and value that concern. But then, ask them to hold you accountable. Explain that helping you become a better leader and a better person is the true definition of caring.

One more thing. It's great to have a partner you can rely on for good, positive feedback, but remember, partners have tough days too. Look for days when it may be your turn to be the "positive advocate."

You may also want to consider the frequency with which you have "one of those days." Your partner is a short-term solution. If "those days" drag into weeks and months, you probably need a more long-term fix. Certainly, regular exercise, a healthful diet, stress reduction techniques, and other forms of self-care are necessities for all of us!

15 Gems of Wisdom to Pass Along as You Mentor the Emerging Leader

Whether your mentee plans a career in business, a role in civic affairs, or a life of family leadership, awareness of the core leadership fundamentals is imperative. Here are some basic thoughts and truths worth talking about:

1. An emerging leader is not capable now of what he or she will be asked to do 15 years from now. We should be challenged by this truth, not frightened.

2. Leadership is an acquired skill, born of personal commitment and discipline over time.

3. Leadership is about clear and specific written instructions with deadlines for completion, measuring results through constant follow-up, and issuing appropriate consequences (positive or negative) for performance (good or bad).

4. Planning is critical. You cannot string together a number of short-term reactions and expect a good result.

5. Leaders organize themselves around a goal and lead from the front.

6. Show up. You can't "call in" leadership. You can't "phone in" real-time direction in the execution phase of a project. Leaders go to the problem or opportunity and have personal impact on the outcome. This is not the same as micro-management.

7. Fifty percent of the leadership leaders get paid to provide is to themselves. Followers get lost when their leaders get lost. Don't neglect your responsibility to put in the time needed to lead yourself.

8. Always put people first. They are your greatest resource. Your people's success and well-being is your greatest priority.

9. Don't ever let someone tell you a high achiever "just needs time" to develop. People learn what we teach. If you sit that star in a corner and come back a year later, you won't see much progress. What works is a carefully considered development plan that is executed by management and monitored by senior leadership.

10. A "sprint, drift, and react" style won't work. Systems rule. No systems means no sustainability.

11. Don't get distracted by the minutiae. Don't get distracted by the wave action above the depths of the ocean.

12. The basic qualities for successful leadership are passion, energy, focus, perseverance, discipline, smarts, a positive attitude, controlled impatience, excellent time management, and "people-bility" (the ability to get buy-in on the effort and have people to do what needs to be done). Honesty is critical if you want long-term success.

13. A successful leader must be competent at four things: 1) understanding concepts and ideas; 2) understanding, managing, and developing people; 3) understanding financial matters, both business and personal; and 4) understanding self-discipline, self-respect, self-confidence, and self-image.

14. Leaders don't leave seating placement to chance. At a meeting or for a business dinner, there is an advantageous place for everyone to sit. The effective leader knows this and directs it.

15. A failed (or failing) leader shows one or more of these fatal flaws:

- Self-promotion ("It's all about me!")
- Arrogance ("You and your ideas don't count!")
- Abrasive style ("My way or the highway!")
- Sloppiness (in behavior, dress, planning, analysis)
- Naivete ("But he said he would…")
- Dishonesty ("Though I was taught 'thou shalt not,' I'm doing it anyway!")
- Uncontrollably bad temper (This is the greatest employee turnover generator.)
- Insecurity ("What can I do to make you like me?")
- Immaturity ("Can you believe the way he acted?")
- Poor grammar and profanity (A great distraction to effective communication)
- Inability to handle money (If you can't handle your money, why should I let you get close to mine?)

So far, we've been talking about the garden-variety type of mentee—leadership candidates who are bright and promising but not exceptional. Sometimes you find an *extraordinary* leadership candidate...so let's switch gears and talk about what it's like to mentor a superstar.

The Exceptional Mentee—Mentoring Someone on the "Fast Track"

Every kind of business has a set of learnable skills that are specific and necessary to success in that business or industry. You must display these skills to be good at what you do in that particular arena.

There is one single skill set, though, that is requisite for success at every leadership position in every industry. That is the ability to communicate and coordinate with all levels and kinds of people and to inspire them to perform successfully the tasks that need to be done...with a smile.

When we find someone with this wonderful attribute—and we see it is also accompanied by other important leadership skills like discipline, hard work, integrity, and "smarts"—we single out this rising star and go to work.

Some folks call this mentoring path the "fast track," although there is nothing especially fast about it. The accelerated learning pace always proceeds at the speed the star can absorb the information and the experience. How fast and how well the person "gets it" is an indication of the magnitude of the star.

The Birth of the "Learn List"

Roger Turner, our division manager over our sprawling I-75 South market, came to me one day and said he had recruited a phenomenal manager trainee. I met the young man and realized he was correct. We had a superstar on our hands. I asked Roger, "What does he need?" Roger replied, "He just needs time." I said, "Great! Let's sit him in a corner for a year and see what we get." That silly but instructive comment was the birth of the Learn List. Knowing this fellow was not going to "drift into greatness," Roger and I sat down together and put on paper everything this potential superstar needed to learn immediately (within 30 days) and what we should teach him in the rest of his first year. The young man got a copy, Roger got a copy, and I kept a copy so I could check progress on the list when I was working in the market. The very effective Learn List is used to this day in the Waffle House development of emerging leaders.

So, let's say you have a rising star on your hands, a real high achiever who has the potential to do big things for your team and your business. How do you effectively develop this person to his or her full potential?

Here is a five-step path I've tried to follow:

1. **First, qualify the candidate.** Don't fall in love with "smooth." Ask yourself what you are really looking at. On a piece of paper or in a digital document, list all the core qualities you appreciate about the candidate. Put down all the strengths you see and also apparent weaknesses you plan to shore up. Start a file with this person's name and place your thoughts in the file. This is a living document you will want to update as new information comes to light.

2. **Sit down with your star and ask him or her about specific plans and goals.** Dig to discover the mentee's true aspirations. What if the dreams are either disappointingly small for the person's potential, naively large, or perhaps incompatible with your mission? It's best to find out early so you can adjust your relationship accordingly. A good probing question to get started might be, "Where do you see yourself in two, five, and ten years?" A much more comprehensive approach is what I

call the "personal reality check" and is discussed earlier in this chapter. The personal reality check is effective in identifying what is most important to a person—the things they really want to do and possess. It separates the "like-to-haves" from the true needs, and it brings to light undesirable outcomes to avoid. A joint conversation about this information will be eye-opening for both of you. Be sure to place a copy of this personal reality check in his or her file.

3. **Make this adage clear to the mentee: "The helping hand you need is often at the end of your very own arm."** Say to your star: "Share with me, please, the details of your self-development plan." No, you don't expect it to be comprehensive, and you certainly won't use it as your development plan for the mentee. But, the answer to this question gives insight into how self-aware and focused the individual is. It also signals the fact that development is a two-way street with as much responsibility residing with the mentee as with the mentor.

4. **If you are directing a program and assigning a mentor for the superstar, choose very wisely. Approach the mentee-mentor match judiciously.** Great players (executors) don't always make good coaches (teachers). The best mentors are good listeners, have a sincere interest in helping other people succeed, show a solid track record of success, possess knowledge and experience in the mentee's specific area of interest, and command peer respect. The last point is critical. The greater the peer respect for your mentor choice, the greater the chances of success for your star.

5. **Carefully manage coordinating the details.** If you are not the mentor, give all the info in the star's file to the person you select. I like to ask my appointed mentors to take a week digging in with the mentee and then prepare their Learn List. Recall that this is the list of things (skills, knowledge, books to be

read, etc.) that your rising high achiever absolutely needs to learn quickly (in the next 30 days) and also over the course of the coming year. Several copies should be made of this plan. The mentee gets one, the mentor gets one, and, of course, you get one. If you are not the actual mentor, it will be critical to follow up and follow progress every month. The more in-volved you are from the sideline, the greater your star's chances for success.

As you move through the mentoring relationship, you will discover more about your mentee with every meeting. You will watch him or her grow in skill and confidence as a result of your efforts and coaching. The books and articles you have given your mentee to read and the "truth-in-life" concepts you have passed along to them will be eye-opening and enlightening. Your continued efforts and counsel will produce for the world an emerging leader, an effective manager, or simply a solid citizen. You should feel fulfilled and very proud for creating so much value in another person's life.

CHAPTER 6

Closing the Loop...and a Few Final Insights for You to Share

"When Is It Over?"

People have asked me how long you should mentor someone. The quick answer is the same one your mother gave you when you asked her, "How will I know when I'm in love?" The answer is..."You will just know."

You will know because one of three things will happen:

1. You'll realize there is practically no more value to add on your watch (the cup is full).

2. You'll suddenly become aware that the effort you are putting in and the advice you are offering is going in one ear and out the other (the cup has a hole in it and will never be more than half full).

3. Your mentee will stop calling for sit-downs or to "just run things by you" (the cup has moved on).

As Sherry will mention in the second half of this book, if you are part of a large mentoring program, there may necessarily be a structured beginning, middle, and end. However, in a one-on-one relationship, the best answer regarding when it's over is "never." This is the answer I always wish for!

I still have contact with men and women who sat across the table from me 40 years ago. At first, we talked about college, then we talked about jobs. Then we talked about surviving and thriving in the business world. Then we talked about marriage and kids and finances and stress. And now we talk about how they are enjoying the fruits of a successful life, playing with their grandchildren, and adding value to other people's lives. No one can doubt this is the perfect outcome.

So, let's say you find that you have taken the mentee as far as you can (or perhaps the full distance you need to take them in your area of expertise) or that the advice and information you gave worked and they have "graduated." What now? Well, you can either say, "Congratulations! Call me if you need me," or you can introduce the mentee to another of your mentor friends who has the chance to add value in a different part of his or her life.

I once mentored an exceptional young lady from another country who wanted some business advice. We talked several times, and I answered all the business questions. Then I realized her most pressing matter was the need to obtain a work visa in her specific occupational specialty. I called a friend who has a much larger Rolodex than I do (for you folks under 40, that's an analog phone directory on a wheel!) and asked him to meet my mentee. We all met for lunch and he brought along an attorney who is an expert in such matters. My friend and the attorney took over on issues beyond my scope.

Regretfully, there are times you realize you are rowing upstream and your mentee is not lifting a paddle. Sometimes it just doesn't work out for other reasons. In such cases, it is perfectly okay to go one of two routes: "tough love" or a graceful exit. If you think the effort is worthwhile, then by all means have a frank talk. But if you honestly think it is a waste of your and the mentee's time, simply tell the mentee you don't think you are "right for him" and wish him well. The owner of one of our largest Waffle House franchise organizations told me once, "Bert, never try to teach a pig to sing. It wastes your time and annoys the pig."

Some Bonus Ideas to Share and Discuss

You may wonder why I have saved these tidbits of truth in life and business for last. It's because the following insights may go a bit beyond the typical mentoring talk. There are times when things just "click." You and the mentee are on the same wavelength. Conversations run a little deeper than with other mentees. You sense the person is truly listening and that what you are saying is resonating. In other words, you find yourself in a conversation that's a little more philosophical than the norm.

At such times, it may seem appropriate to initiate a more nuanced discussion on the nature of leadership, what success really means, how to be a better person, and so forth. Go ahead. Dig deep and share some of the insights you've acquired over a lifetime. (You may even find the energy of the conversation allows these insights to coalesce in your own mind in a way they haven't before. This is one of the gifts of mentoring!)

To follow are a few of the insights I acquired in my Waffle House career. Some of them are not "obvious" statements, and that is by design. They are meant to evoke pondering and deeper discussion. Feel free to share them with your mentee (assuming you agree) and to add your own insights.

About Leadership

The price of impact is criticism.

Companion management is adding people to make yourself more comfortable. Don't do it.

Knowing is not doing. Talk is not work. Information is not execution.

When the meeting gets off point, say, "We are not here to discuss everything; this is an impact meeting."

Often when good ideas go bad, the opportunity or the concept didn't change. The leadership changed.

When businesses fail because of misguided leadership, they usually go down in history as a clear case of financial suicide driven by ego and preference.

The trick in leadership is to drive "good" and don't allow "bad." This is the same as "reward what you like and punish what you don't like."

All voices are not equal. Listen for constructive voices that have a history of validity and value.

When there is a vacuum of information, people make things up.

Strategy is where you want to be; planning and tactics are how you get there.

Yesterday won't lead you to tomorrow. It's important to be a student of history, but the "history will tell you" approach to leadership is management by looking over your shoulder.

When planning any great effort, don't think randomly. Start by defining all the important categories that make a difference and then list the details under each that are requisite to success.

When reading an analysis, be alert that someone may simply be trying to talk you into something.

The success of the average person will not exceed his leadership. Energetic, resourceful, high achievers with curiosity are the exception. They can exceed and even outpace the leader.

You can't make progress if you routinely debate the validity of proven fundamentals.

Failing companies usually leave their customers long before their customers leave them.

What works long-term is a sustained commitment to fundamentals.

When you don't like what you see, the role of active intervention is better than the role of passive tolerance.

"Overwhelmed" is a temporary emotion born of a lack of organization, direction, or delegation.

Every organization has critical, "make it or break it" areas, the unwatched metrics of which can head south in a hurry. What are your categories for vigilance?

About Success

A successful life is about adding value.

You cannot chase happiness and success. We attract it by the person we become.

—From Jim Rohn, loosely quoted

A lot of the roads you travel in life aren't paved.

There are speed bumps in progress. Until you hit a few, you don't know how you're doing.

Give accurate, direct answers. Don't exaggerate and don't hedge. You'll be respected if you do this and thought incompetent if you don't.

Success is not about personal preference but about what works. Given a choice between wishful theory or experience and reality, take the latter.

Regarding hard work, the first 40 hours are very competitive. At 50 and 60 hours a week, the crowd thins out quite a bit.

Be alert from whom you take advice. Jobs and titles don't create, of their own account, knowledge and wisdom.

Most people have a hard time getting from where they are to where they want to be if there is pain and suffering along the way.

All roads are not straight. That's why they put up guardrails.

The road to failure frequently starts by traveling down the road of personal preference.

The unsuccessful person can usually be identified with a group.

Every man (and woman) needs to make up his mind if he's going to succeed. This will require him to act differently from the alternative.

Ninety-nine percent of our success is about showing up and executing.

The key component in the personal success equation is not what you do but rather who you are in business with.

Intent is not a system, and hope is not a strategy.

—From Rudy Giuliani, loosely quoted

About Personal Life

Bad habits and bad behavior may not have immediate bad consequences. Sometimes it takes a while to stumble through death's door.

Being able to balance your life has more to do with you than with your business.

You try a lot of things in life. Some of them work. Some don't. Learn to live with it.

Be aware that emotional cycles are inevitable in life, for you and for everyone else.

Debt is not an emotional issue. It is a mathematical issue. Debt must be guided by awareness and thought, not passion and hope.

Stay away from the risk cliff.

The goal is to do the most good for the largest number of people over the longest period of time.

There is a difference between just thinking and being really good at it.

Don't confuse discipline with stubbornness.

Irritation is the seed of opportunity.

There is a human perception that things are either easier today or tougher today. The truth is that the challenges are simply different.

A crowd is a good thing to lead, not to follow.

You grow or you shrink relative to your surroundings. Nothing stays the same.

You may not be able to immediately change the stressful situations in your life but you are unilaterally in control of how you react to them.

About the Way the World Works

"People don't care how much you know until they know how much you care."

—Theodore Roosevelt

Never build arguments based on exceptions to the norm.

When in doubt, bet on human nature.

In basically a prosperous civilization, why are we fighting about all these things?

Why do we elect people who act surprised about anything?

There is a lot of conversation about restaurants. Nothing has changed in the food industry. They still sell calories. They are just trying to make the calories more interesting.

Be aware of real-world limitations. Some things you can't do any more than you can repeal the law of gravity.

Pride of ownership is a powerful thing. Nobody washes a rental car.

Gratitude not refreshed turns into entitlement, and if not dealt with, entitlement turns into resentment.

"Whatever limits us we call Fate."

—Ralph Waldo Emerson

"God does not play dice with the Universe."

—Albert Einstein

One of the problems people frequently have is that they think in ruts.

—From Zig Ziglar, loosely quoted

Where is it written that we must be consistent?

Pleasure and happiness are different breeds of the same dog.

—From Josh Billings, loosely quoted

Just because people don't understand something does not mean it won't work.

And, finally...an anecdote about optimism and pessimism:

The CEOs of two competing shoe companies sent their top salesmen to the African Congo to open a new market. After the first day, both salesmen sized up the market and each sent an email to his respective CEO. The first salesman wrote, "Coming home tomorrow. Nobody wears shoes here." The second salesman wrote, "Send extra help. Nobody wears shoes here."

CHAPTER 7

Epilogue to Part 1 (Bert's Advice)

For my part in this book, I have tried to point out that the act of being a mentor to someone—that is, coaching and helping them to be the more valuable person they want to become—is a wonderful thing for both parties. But the role of mentor is not necessarily meant for everyone. There are many other ways to help people along the path to success in life, including financial help, written recommendations, and even suggestions on who would be an appropriate mentor for them. I've done all of these things, and by far, mentoring is the most labor-intensive and time-consuming…yet also the most rewarding.

If mentoring is the task you intend to undertake, be prepared for hard (but very enjoyable) work. For your reference, here is a summary of some key points I've made in the previous pages:

- Qualify yourself. Make sure you have the time, patience, and commitment for the effort this role requires.
- Qualify the mentee candidate. Ensure a good fit for your effort.

- Size up the job ahead. Your starting point may be "personal" rather than "professional."
- Your coaching venture will likely include a combination of education, inspiration, motivation, and relationship-brokering.
- There are many helpful tools to aid you in your endeavor and successful ways to approach the challenge of mentoring. Make use of them.
- Figure out the central truths you've learned in your career and life and share them with your mentee. I've identified five critical concepts you may want to pass along during your time together. I believe your mentee's understanding of them will significantly enhance his or her chances for long-term success. I invite you to share them as you see fit, along with your own lessons and insights, of course.
- There is nothing fast about the "fast track." If you have a star on your hands, it's less about speed and more about focused effort on his or her part and yours.
- Not everyone is meant to be a superstar. Sometimes you just need to coach someone on how to be an effective professional and human being.
- Hopefully the personal relationship will last long after the heavy-lifting work of mentoring is done. If not, there will be ample signs to let you know your work is complete.

If you are working inside an organization that you know would benefit from a structured mentoring program, I urge you to continue with the second half of this book. Even if not, you may wish to read it anyway. It provides a different perspective on mentoring from the section you have just read, and I believe it will actually reinforce your passion for taking on this work.

Finally, be grateful for the opportunity to share your knowledge and insights with others, to help them see themselves, their lives, their potential, and their future in a new way. I believe we are all here to love one another. Love isn't just a feeling we have. It's action we take. It's putting forth time, effort, and energy for the growth and betterment of others. Love and mentoring are not always easy, but that's what makes them worth doing.

GOODBYE, BERT; HELLO, SHERRY

The "Bridge" Between Parts 1 and 2

I am not a writer by nature; I'm a talker. I spent a career at Waffle House talking to people across a booth table — directing, instructing, offering advice, and mentoring. So, when I talk with you, the reader, that's how I write: just like we are having a conversation over breakfast.

Dr. Sherry Hartnett comes from a different swatch of cloth. As founding director of the University of West Florida's Executive Mentor Program and owner of a marketing and leadership consulting company, she works in both academic and corporate environments. She regularly talks to people in board rooms and business meetings and writes strategic plans, executive summaries, informational updates, and after-action reports. Her part of the book reflects the style of thinking and writing required in such situations. In short, Sherry writes differently (and better) than I do.

I say all of this to explain why the two parts of this book have such very different tones. But you may be wondering how two such very different people ended up collaborating on a book in the first place. Here's the answer:

The practice of mentoring is informal. It's conversational. You might even describe it as improvisational. But to maximize the power of mentoring inside an organization, there does need to be some structure around it. As I continued to hear from people what a valuable tool mentoring is, I became more and more convinced the book needed to address how to operationalize it—how to make it a regular part of how the organization does things.

That's where Sherry comes in. She takes my Part 1 advice about effectively mentoring one-on one and offers direction about how to turn that into a successful, sizeable program in a large organization. Yes, her style is different from mine, but that's a good thing.

Together, I hope we have made a great team for you in this effort to bring comprehensive answers to the two questions posed by leaders in organizations of all sizes: *How can I personally mentor most effectively?* and *How would I successfully scale-up that skill to maximize positive impact in my company?*

Read on to explore how Sherry put into place the extremely successful Executive Mentor Program that serves both the University of West Florida and the city of Pensacola, Florida. And get ready to think about how you can do the same in your organization, given her advice and instruction.

Welcome, Sherry…and thank you for joining us.

—Bert

PART 2

SHERRY'S ADVICE

Mentoring: A Powerful Tool to Retain Key Employees and Grow Tomorrow's Leaders

"Iron sharpens iron, and one man sharpens another."

—*The Bible, Proverbs 27:17*

As Bert mentioned earlier, a successful mentoring relationship can positively change a life. Just as certainly, a well-executed mentoring program can have the same positive impact on an organization, whether it is a large corporation, a not-for-profit, or a college within a university.

So, you want to fire up a mentoring program that will transform your organization? That's great news! Peter Drucker said, "Management is doing things right; leadership is doing the right things." (Drucker) And mentoring *is* the right thing. It's one of the most powerful tools for preparing tomorrow's leaders as well as keeping established leaders up to speed on current tools and technologies. (Remember, reverse mentoring is a growing trend!)

Seven Great Benefits of Reverse Mentoring

A great reverse mentoring program will allow your company to...

1. Empower emerging leaders by letting them see how their work is valued.

2. Embrace new-age skills such as digital and social media. This will help you to drive your company's digital transformation (which has now become a "must-have" rather than a "nice-to-have.")

3. Close generational gaps and break down stereotypes. Reverse mentoring creates better understanding and empathy, which in turn improves collaboration and teamwork.

4. Increase retention of millennials by providing the recognition they seek from management.

5. Drive culture change through gaining new perspectives and multi-generational insights.

6. Give your company a fresh perspective, improving leadership and communication skills.

7. Better understand emerging social responsibility values. This is crucial for creating a culture that attracts young, purpose-driven talent and framing your products and services as socially responsible.

Bert covered many of the benefits of mentoring in the Introduction to this book. I agree with all of his insights. But here, I want to highlight just a few that I see over and over.

First and foremost, mentoring is a proven approach to drive productive learning and personal development. People need solid, relevant training, and mentoring programs provide it. They also benefit the organization by keeping key employees engaged, establishing a succession plan, and building a strong bench. Mentoring programs increase commitment to the organization, improve communication, and generate the development of managers.

Gallup data shows that only 17 percent of millennials report routine meaningful feedback from their managers. (Hickman) This is a significant oversight. People hunger for feedback and they need it more than once a year. A mentor can deliver some of that missing interaction, validation, and guidance, especially mentors who mentees see as experts. Mentors can provide a push to employees to not only perform better in their present jobs but also to take on learning something new, pursuing professional development, or getting involved in industry events.

When done well—when the mentors connect to the individual mentee's needs, abilities, and aspirations—a mentoring program can have a more significant impact on leader development than more generalized leadership training. This is great news for organizations operating on a "lean and mean" budget that might not have extensive training funds.

"As a leader, I find that mentoring is helpful to get a better understanding of the workers entering my workplace and making sure I can meet their needs."

—UWF former executive mentor Bentina Chisolm Terry, senior vice president, region external affairs and community engagement, Georgia Power

Mentoring Is a Powerhouse Tool for Employee Retention

Many companies face a competitive marketplace. Companies that foster stronger relationships with employees are in a better position to attract and retain talent. Employees need to know the company they are working for is interested in their professional growth and development. This fundamental thought has prompted many a forward-thinking company to launch a formal mentoring program.

Helping employees grow in their careers is no longer nice to have; it's a must-have. According to LinkedIn's 2019 Workplace Learning Report ("Workplace Learning Report"), more than nine in ten employees would stay at a company longer if their employers invested in their careers by helping them learn.

It can be difficult and expensive to replace great employees. Employers can spend 33 percent (Sears) of a worker's annual salary on hiring a new replacement. And, when companies lose top talent, there is also lost opportunity, morale, reputation, customer relationships, and other intangibles that are harder to measure. Mentoring will keep your high performers from looking elsewhere.

This is important because high performers are your company's most valuable resource. These are the employees who bring the most significant value to your business—and to your customers—so it pays to do whatever you can to keep them happy, engaged and with your company for the long run. Julie Lodge-Jarrett, former chief talent officer for Ford Motor Co., put it best in a *Wall Street Journal* article in which she said, "People aren't going to be willing to tolerate an employer, regardless of how good the pay is, or how stable the job is, if they're not happy." (Cutter and Feintzeig)

```
┌─────────────────────────────┐
│        NAVY FEDERAL         │
│        CASE STUDY           │
└─────────────────────────────┘
```

Mentorship Program at Navy Federal Credit Union Yields Return on Investment

Navy Federal Credit Union is a stellar example of a large, worldwide organization with a robust mentorship program. To give you a sense of their size, they have more than 18,000 employees, 9 million members, 330 locations worldwide, and $125 billion in assets.

Navy Federal leadership believes that one of the most effective ways to increase employee engagement and retention while providing an incredible development opportunity is through mentorship.

"Establishing the mentorship program is a business decision that has an entirely positive impact," says Thomas Greek, vice president of learning and development at Navy Federal Credit Union. He adds, "The best part is that mentoring utilizes the resources that your company already has and yields an incredible ROI." And while Navy Federal's internal stats on the program are confidential, Greek describes their program's ROI as "*highly* successful by our internal standards."

One way mentoring retains high performers is by keeping them engaged and giving them visibility through connections with other high performers and members of your executive team. A big reason these employees excel is that they're smart, active, and curious—they are always looking for something new and stimulating to do. Satisfy that need by providing them with the opportunity to participate in your mentoring program.

Mentoring is stimulating, not only for rising junior-level employees but also for high-performing senior talent. You can help them keep their passion burning strong, giving them an opportunity to share their wisdom. As senior leaders mentor younger folks, they learn from them as well. Even if it's not a formal reverse mentoring program, the give and take will benefit both parties.

Creating and nourishing a huge pool of high performers is great for your company in general. Great performers lift the entire team by resetting standards of behavior and productivity and generating a ripple effect that can influence everyone in your workplace. They create an atmosphere of commitment and ownership that's catching and will impact everyone around them and elevate your brand. And soon, you'll have a pool of potential new leaders within your company.

Mentoring Programs Can Forge Relationships Between Companies and Universities

In addition to providing a wealth of advantages to students, a mentorship program is an excellent way for universities to develop relationships with professionals who previously might have had little or no connection to that university. Sometimes this initial connection leads professionals to support or assist the university.

"If you're looking for a way to engage alumni, community leaders, and students, there is no better way than to start a mentoring program," says James Hosman, UWF alumnus and executive mentor, and market president of Centennial Bank. "Alumni and community leaders like to take pride in their local university and pass experiences along to students. Additionally, this is a fantastic way to place top-level students into local businesses.

"All but one of my prior mentees are working with local businesses that I helped make a connection to," he adds. "By no means am I saying I got them the job; that was all the mentees' doing, but their having an advocate in the local community certainly helped. No better way to keep talent local than to introduce them to opportunities before graduation!"

Mentor/mentee relationships exist even in the highest echelons of business. One of the world's most successful and richest men, Bill Gates, benefits from having a mentor, Warren Buffett. "Warren isn't just a great friend. He is also an amazing mentor. I have been learning from him since the day we met in 1991. We discuss business, economics, politics, world events, and of course, philanthropy," said Gates in his Gates Notes blog. (Gates)

Mentoring Program Q&A: The Fundamentals to Know Before You Get Started

A thriving mentoring program is within your reach. But they don't just happen on their own. Before you get to work, you need to know why you're doing it and the benefits you expect to receive. Only when you understand these essentials can you build a well-executed program through thoughtful planning and a sustained commitment to guiding participants through the mentoring process.

Here, in Q&A format, are a few fundamentals to keep in mind before putting your mentoring program together.

- **What is mentoring, anyway?** It's a personal, helping relationship between a mentor and mentee that includes professional development and growth and varying degrees of support. A mentoring program based on mutual respect creates a supportive environment, fosters trust, and facilitates information-sharing. In this learning journey, effective mentoring encourages and nurtures mentees by enhancing their knowledge, expertise, and attitudes, enabling them to grow and develop.
- **Is there a difference between mentoring and coaching?** Yes! Mentoring facilitates broad development and career progress, whereas coaching addresses skills in some aspects of an individual's work. The time frame for

mentoring is for long-term growth, whereas coaching is typically for short-term performance. And, mentoring emphasizes counseling, supporting, and introducing, while coaching is more concerned with providing practical application and teaching skills.

- **What functions does the mentor provide?** Mentors provide role modeling, advice, and friendship to the mentee. They support the mentee in developing a sense of competence, confidence, and effectiveness. Mentors act as teachers, guides, exemplars, counselors, and supporters—but most importantly, they assist and facilitate the realization of the mentee's goals and dreams.

Three Mentor "Musts"

To make a positive impact, my research (Hartnett) shows that mentors must:

1. Display role model behavior and a willingness to share their expertise

2. Provide support and encouragement with sincerity, openness, and honesty

3. Deploy networking and relationship-building skills

Three Mentee "Musts"

For mentees to thrive in a mentorship program, they must have:

1. The motivation to succeed

2. The willingness to learn

3. A positive attitude

Bert's section of the book provides more insights into the role of mentors and mentees.

- **WIIFM? (So, what's in it for me?)** Let me ask you this: Do you want to better engage and drive up the performance of your employees? Would you like to make your workplace more attractive to potential job seekers? Are you anxious to retain and energize your high performers? If your answer is yes to any of those questions, a mentoring program will be an important part of your ongoing business plan.

   It's also worth noting that as the leader who establishes a mentoring program, you will get a good bit of credit for the outcomes the program provides, like creating more high performers and retaining talent. Also, if you serve as a mentor in the program, you get a lot of personal satisfaction from impacting another person's life in a positive way.

- **What are the most regularly mentioned positive outcomes for mentees?** The benefits to mentees include support, encouragement, help with subject knowledge resources, sharing ideas and advice, feedback/positive reinforcement, increased confidence, and career affirmation/commitment. Additionally, mentees develop positive and confident self-images. Mentorship aids them in learning the organizational ropes, developing a sense of competence and effectiveness, and learning how to behave in management roles with increasing responsibility.

   Working with a mentor also provides employees the opportunity to develop a network with a broad range of people, which means more resources and career opportunities. This can be significant in kick-starting a mentee's career.

"Having a mentor has been a great networking opportunity for me," says Gabriel Glaysher, mortgage loan officer at Emerald Mortgage Corporation and former mentee of the UWF Executive Mentor Program. "When a CEO of a company can meet with me for an hour and focus entirely on helping me succeed in my career, it demonstrates how much my mentor cares."

Social Capital Pays Off for Mentors and Mentees

Think of networking as social capital, says mentoring expert and coauthor of *Strategic Relationships at Work*, Dr. Wendy Murphy, Babson College:

"Social capital doesn't exist within the individual; it exists in a network," she says. "It's how we build relationships that help us get our jobs done, because none of us work in a vacuum. Mentoring is one way of working through social capital. Participating in a program like the one at the University of West Florida is one step in accumulating that social capital you need.

"Make no mistake; it's work," continues Dr. Murphy. "It takes energy to sustain relationships. It takes energy to meet new people. It takes energy to stay in touch with them. But it is entirely worth it. Not only will your career be better, but you'll make others' careers better as well." (Murphy)

- **What factors help a mentoring program succeed?** Successful mentoring programs thrive with organizational support, clarity of purpose, the participants' commitment to the program, careful selection and matching procedures, and continuous monitoring and evaluation.
- **On the other hand, what are the main reasons mentoring programs fail?** There are many factors that can trip up mentoring programs and cause them to fail. For example:
  - Not enough buy-in at the top
  - The program thrown together by overextended and overwhelmed people who've never built a mentoring program
  - Relying too much on mentoring software and not enough on personal relationships

- Not promoting a program well internally
- Not training participants enough
- Underestimating the time and effort needed to make meaningful matches
- Too much structure
- Not enough structure
- Mandating that people participate

- **Can my company afford a mentoring program?** Too many organizations see the benefits of mentoring but tell themselves they can't afford it. But when you consider the benefits enumerated in this chapter, the real question is, *Can they afford not to?* You can start a mentoring program within your budget (even if that budget is zero). There are a lot of different options, and one of them is most likely right for your company.

  The recommended option is to hire a program manager and invest in the program expenses, but you don't have to go that route. You could hire an outside consultant for a set period of time to focus on implementing a new program. You could invest in online mentoring software; however, you still need someone on staff to manage the program. The zero-cost option is you can do it yourself or assign it to one of your superstar leaders. With this option, you must consider the person's mentoring expertise and the lost productivity time if someone is pulled away from other responsibilities. Regardless of which option you choose, the payoff is almost always well worth it.

Once you've taken the time to digest the above information, it's time to get to the nuts and bolts of starting a program that will strengthen your organization for years to come. The upcoming chapters provide you comprehensive assistance as you plan, establish, and grow a mentoring program. They are based on the seven vital steps to creating a robust mentoring program:

Step 1: Define Your "Why"

Step 2: Find Your Program Champion

Step 3: Set Goals and Metrics

Step 4: Build Your Program

Step 5: Recruit and Connect

Step 6: Nurture Your People and Your Program

Step 7: Measure to Improve

✓ Success Secret: Use This Book as a Step-by-Step Practical Guide to Building Your Program

Within each section, examples from the University of West Florida's Executive Mentor Program are included for consideration for your mentoring program.

I have found these seven steps to be a great, workable framework for my clients and for me. The steps are easy to understand, step-by-step, not overwhelming, achievable, and practical. I invite you to read on...and it's my sincere hope that you put what you learn into practice inside your organization.

"Holy Bible." The New American Version ed., J. G. Ferguson Publishing Company, 1971.

"Workplace Learning Report." 3rd ed., 2019, p. 38. general editor, LinkedIn.

Cutter, Chip and Rachel Feintzeig. "Smile! Your Boss Is Tracking Your Happiness." *Wall Street Journal*, 2020, March 6, 2020. *wsj.com*.

Drucker, Peter F. *The Essential Drucker: The Best of Sixty Years of Peter Drucker's Essential Writings on Management.* Routledge, 2000.

Gates, Bill. "50 Years of Warren's Wisdom." *gatesnotes.com*, 2015.

Hartnett, Sherry. "The Effects of a Business Executive Mentoring Program on College Students: A Study on Augmenting Workforce Readiness Capacity." *International Engaged Management Scholarship Conference*, 2016.

Hickman, Adam. "What 'Meaningful Feedback' Means to Millennials." *Gallup Workplace*, 2020.

Murphy, Wendy. "Propelling Women's Careers: A Developmental Network Approach." *Women in Leadership Conference*, University of West Florida, 2017.

Sears, Lindsay. "Retention Report: Trends, Reasons, & Recommendations." 2017, p. 9. general editor, Work Institute.

CHAPTER 8

Step 1: Define Your "Why"

If you are reading this book, you are likely either the owner or a senior leader of your company. CEOs and top executives tend to be the people who approach me for help with their mentoring program as they avidly look to move their organization forward. Human resources executives reach out in some cases, motivated by knowing that a mentoring program could be a game changer to both the employees and the company's bottom line.

You might also be a reader employed at a college or university. Higher education has a two-fold interest in mentoring programs: student success and increased funding. First, mentoring programs can empower students to get jobs, specifically high-paying ones. This is what parents want, what students want, and what higher education leaders want. Second, as a result, some states such as Florida have a policy providing a portion of state funding for public colleges and universities based on their performance in this arena. Specifically, colleges are often judged, among other things, on how many graduates are employed within one year and what their median wages are. Anecdotal evidence suggests that college mentorship programs improve these employment and wage outcomes.

If you're employed by a college, these two reasons are sufficient reasons to be excited about being involved in a mentoring program for your students. If you're employed in the private sector, you'll need to get more intentional about articulating your "why." Having enthusiasm and excitement for your upcoming mentoring program is fantastic. Still, if you don't clearly identify your program's purpose up front, you will likely not realize ongoing success. As Amanda Schnieders says in *Entrepreneur*, "While mentoring for the sake of mentoring checks the good-deed box, it isn't enough to create sustainable impact." (Schnieders)

In the previous chapter, we talked about some of the benefits of mentoring programs in general. There are many great reasons to implement one. But now it's time to look at *your* company and its unique needs. What do you want your program to achieve? Do you want to...

- Develop a robust multi-level succession plan?
- Prepare an employee to take on a larger leadership role?
- Increase the number of women or minority employees in leadership positions?
- Retain talented employees?
- Onboard high-potential new employees?

Navigating the culture, internal politics, traditions, and relationships in a new organization can be the most difficult—and frustrating—part of adjusting to and succeeding in a new position. Less experienced employees need all the help they can get!

When we define the "why," we accomplish several goals at once. First and foremost, of course, knowing the "why" will help you shape a successful program that meets the needs of the organization and its employees and, if you're in higher education, the stakeholders affiliated with the school. But it will also allow you to:

- Confidently convince stakeholders the program is needed by putting some hard numbers in front of them.
- Create a sense of urgency for getting the program off the ground and keeping the momentum going.
- Get buy-in at every level. This includes getting people to serve as mentors and to sign on as mentees. When people understand the "why" behind what you're trying to do, they are more likely not just to comply, but to throw their full enthusiasm behind it.

The first step to determining the "why" is to ask questions to understand the need. You must be clear about your goals and tailor the overall mentoring program to specific objectives in your business plan. Your company may need to fix a problem or simply develop your people. And there doesn't have to be anything "wrong." As John F. Kennedy said in his State of the Union address in 1962, "The time to repair the roof is when the sun is shining." (Kennedy)

One of the simplest yet most effective ways to ask these questions is to hold meetings with the executive team to determine where the company needs help. Just ensure you make decisions based on facts and data, not assumptions. Employee satisfaction surveys can provide some indication of where there are needs. Still, one of the best ways to truly learn about employee wants and needs is during one-on-one meetings with their supervisors as they have ongoing performance conversations and performance reviews.

BIG QUESTION 1: What will be improved for our organization?

Some of the questions you will want to ask yourself and other leaders will aim to uncover what needs work in your organization. (If we are truly holding up the mirror, we can usually find at least a few things that need attention and improvement.) Therefore, it is important to be brutally honest in answering these questions:

- Why do we need a mentoring program?
- Where are we struggling? What goals do we need to improve on?
- What problem(s) are we trying to solve that a mentoring program might help with? What are the benefits to our company? To our employees?
- Why did I pick up this book?

You might be thinking your company culture needs improvement. Mentoring programs can play a vital role. While culture is intangible, it can be felt when the right actions come together. Mentors' actions are highly visible and positively reinforce the overall culture that leaders want to create.

Again, for an organization that is doing fine, this can be your opportunity to elevate performance. But for an organization that is struggling, these questions will illuminate issues that can be addressed and improved through your mentoring program.

COX COMMUNICATIONS
CASE STUDY

Knowing Their "Why," Cox
Offers Several Mentoring Programs

Cox Communications is an excellent example of a company that understands "why" they invest in mentoring programs. With more than 18,000 employees, Cox provides advanced digital video, Internet, telephone, and home security and automation services over its nationwide IP network.

Kia Painter, senior vice president, HR business partnerships at Cox Communications, says, "Mentoring has been a great avenue for creating connections among executives and emerging talent." She stressed that, "Building relationships is an important competency for all leaders, and mentoring helps all flex muscles in this area."

To achieve their "why" of building stronger relationships among leaders and staff, Cox offers several mentoring programs.

- Executive
- Peer-to-Peer
- New Hire (Buddy)
- Reverse Mentoring—which also strengthens digital transformation
- Mentoring Circles—which are leveraged by their Employee Resource Groups to foster allyship among different diverse groups of employees

At universities, mentoring students is proven to improve retention and boost the percentage of students who gain jobs in their fields upon graduation. Since its 2012 founding, the Executive Mentor Program at the University of West Florida (UWF) College of Business has made a positive impact on campus and in Northwest Florida.

> UWF
> **CASE STUDY**

Our "Why" at UWF: Closing the Workplace Readiness Gap

Between talking with business executives in our community and analyzing national research on the topic, we knew college graduates entering the workforce typically have the technical or hard skills, such as those associated with accounting, economics, or marketing. However, they often lack soft skills, or as I like to say, "human skills," the intangible personal characteristics associated with *success*, such as communication, team-building, critical-thinking, professionalism, and self-confidence.

Workforce readiness in college students occurs when graduates have a combination of social, personal, and applied cognitive skills. Nationwide, however, business leaders grumble they often feel forced to hire candidates who fall short on interpersonal abilities, especially young workers more accustomed to texting than talking. This gap between employer requirements and college graduates with the desired workforce competencies has negatively impacted new graduates' ability to obtain and succeed in professional positions in their fields, with 60 percent or less, nationally, getting jobs in their field after graduation. That's a problem.

We identified this workforce readiness gap in intangible "human skills" as what we wanted to improve and the reason to establish the Executive Mentor Program. We had found our "why."

My research (Hartnett) on the effects of a mentoring program on college students and how it can augment workforce readiness capacity revealed these practical implications for leaders managing in the workplace:

- The intangible "soft skills" of professionalism, communication, leadership, critical-thinking, and self-confidence are significant in forming workforce readiness.
- There is a positive relationship between effective mentoring and workforce readiness.
- Business executives who act as mentors and support mentees in their personal and professional growth help mentees gain the soft skills for successful careers.
- Not surprisingly, the soft-skills issue is not limited to the United States. I spoke with professionals from throughout the world who agreed: This is a global issue and a mentoring opportunity. There is value in pairing business executives and leaders with soon-to-be graduating students and

current employees to provide them with a competitive edge and improve their chances for success in their work careers.

These realizations have fueled my enthusiasm for our Executive Mentor Program at UWF, and motivated me to share our story and the how-tos of successful mentorship as broadly as possible.

Two Crucial Insights from a Mentoring Master

As I continue to read, conduct research, and talk to experts in the field of mentoring, executive mentor Michael Ryan shared with me his book *Make Your Career Go BOOM! Not Bust: Practical Tips to Succeed in an Ever-Changing World.* During our thought-provoking follow-up conversation about it, two points he made really stood out to me. Point one is that mentorship programs lead to successful students (and happy parents). Point two is that mentors provide objective, honest feedback that students can't get anywhere else.

"With so much pressure on universities not only to educate students but to ensure they gain employment afterward, a mentorship program can provide their students a competitive edge," says Ryan. "Mentors can share valuable practical tools that students can utilize not only in landing a job but in succeeding in it. As college deans know: happy parents, happy life."

He continues, "It is crucial for students to have a credible person or persons they can turn to for honest advice. Too often, friends or family 'pull their punches' because they don't want to offend or alienate a person. A mentor can provide a student with his or her insights and offer them different ways to look at an idea or a decision. Sometimes a student will share with a mentor their true feelings that they are reluctant to share with others. Often there is a bonding between the mentor and the mentee."

I know you will find similar success with your mentoring program after going through the seven steps described in this book. Creating a mentoring program is a meaningful and worthwhile endeavor that will reward you as much as it rewards the mentees and mentors who will bring your program to life.

BIG QUESTION 2: Why would our employees benefit from a mentoring program?

Whether someone has worked for 20 years or is brand new to the workforce, it can be challenging to navigate the intricacies of a career. It is also important to remember that every organization has its own challenges and quirks. One doesn't always learn in school or books about the internal culture and politics, unique processes, and opportunities within a company. Nor does education prepare people for the small steps and learnings that lead to different phases of their professional career. Carefully planned mentoring programs help employees bridge these problematic gaps in training and help them thrive.

The goal of the Navy Federal mentorship program, for example, is to enhance the development of employees (mentees) through paired relationships with their senior-leader mentors. The program provides individuals with one-to-one partnering that enhances the growth of both the mentee and the mentor. This focused attention on professional development provides an opportunity for mentees to reflect and develop with their mentors. The mentee's development depends on exploring career aspirations, strengths and weaknesses, collaborating on means to "get there," implementing strategies, and evaluating along the way.

And let's not overlook the tremendous benefit of fostering employee satisfaction. This is one way mentors can make a significant impact. Having a mentor—someone who can be a guide, a motivator, and an advocate—can increase employee enthusiasm, happiness, personal and professional growth, and retention.

You can assume that these benefits are true for your company. Yet still, in establishing the "why," it's a good idea to go straight to the horse's mouth. Ask your employees probing questions around where they are struggling:

- Do you fully understand your job?
- Does your direct manager provide the support you need?
- Do you know what is needed to meet your goals and objectives?

Ask your employees—especially your top performers:

- Do you feel valued for your contributions?
- Do you feel you are growing professionally?
- Do you feel that your job allows you to develop new skills?
- Do you see a path to advance your career on our team?

As you begin your questioning process, your natural impulse may be to focus on younger or newer employees. This is understandable. However, don't impose limits. Include some employees who have been around for a while. They, too, might benefit from mentoring.

"Many people assume that they need a mentor only when they are first starting out in their careers. We used to think it was people at early stages of their career who needed mentoring, those just out of MBA programs. Now we understand that people at every stage benefit from this kind of assistance," says Dr. Kathy Kram, author of *Mentoring at Work*. (Kram)

After questioning leaders and employees, hopefully you will have a much stronger understanding of why your company needs a good mentorship program. Be sure to capture everyone's responses and write them up sooner rather than later. (We all know how quickly the passage of time blurs the nuances in our memories.) You will need them later as you present your business case, set goals, build your program, and begin to recruit and connect mentors and mentees.

Hopefully, answering these questions has given you some insight into what you want to achieve, why it matters, and how it will positively change your organization. You likely have a sense of urgency to launch your program. Now it's time to find your champion. Read on to learn all about choosing the right person to head up your mentoring program.

"The Labor Market for Recent College Graduates." Federal Reserve Bank of New York, 2021.

Hartnett, Sherry. "The Effects of a Business Executive Mentoring Program on College Students: A Study on Augmenting Workforce Readiness Capacity." *International Engaged Management Scholarship Conference*, 2016.

Kennedy, John F. "Annual Message to the Congress on the State of the Union." JFK Library, 1962.

Kram, Kathy E. *Mentoring at Work: Developmental Relationships in Organizational Life*. University Press of America, Incorporated, 1988.

Schnieders, Amanda. "Why Workplace Mentoring Programs Fail." 2018.

CHAPTER 9

Step 2: Find Your Program Champion

Please take a moment to revisit Bert's parable at the beginning of this book about the origins of (in gorilla speak) MEN-TOR-SHIP. Part of the story centered on gorilla chief Jefe's poor decision to turn over leadership of the program to Blazer, a gorilla famous for his aggressive, "get it done" attitude. As you'll now recall, that didn't work out so well. Jefe eventually came to his senses and reassigned the program to the "great organizer, Sherilla." (Thanks, Bert, I'm flattered!)

Much like Jefe, you will need to choose a champion to head up your mentoring program. In this chapter, we will cover some of the characteristics you will likely want your champion to possess. First, though, let's talk about the role of the champion.

The mentoring champion heads up efforts to get the program started, launched, and running smoothly. They build your program, leading the way by setting goals with senior leaders and creating materials and resources. They recruit, match, and train mentors and mentees. Importantly, they also promote, nurture, and improve the mentoring program continually, always working to ensure results.

To get your mentoring program up and running quickly and well, I recommend one of two options. Either hire a full-time program champion or select a division/department leader to be the program champion with their team's support so the workload can be divided and prioritized among multiple people. Occasionally, I hear of some organizations adding all the responsibilities of the program champion as an add-on role to someone's current job. Truthfully, these are some of the people whom I find to be struggling. It takes time and focus to create, maintain, and continue to improve a robust mentoring program.

In terms of desirable characteristics, the leader you select should be someone who knows the potential mentors and potential mentees who will participate in the program. Understandably, in a large corporation, it would be difficult for one person to know every mentee if they are coming from, say, 20 or 30 different departments. Therefore, the program champion should be a good judge of character, someone who quickly and easily establishes rapport with others.

The right fit will need to be a connector with a welcoming personality who has the time to focus on building a strong mentoring program. At the core of mentoring is the art of fostering meaningful connections. Some people just seem to know everyone and can connect people and their ideas with ease. Through their relationships, they're able to "connect the dots" between people and opportunities and bring them together.

What Is a Connector?

In his international bestseller *The Tipping Point*, Malcolm Gladwell describes Connectors as the people who know large numbers of other people and enjoy making introductions. Gladwell attributes the success of Connectors to the fact that "...their ability to span many different worlds is a function of something intrinsic to their personality, some combination of curiosity, self-confidence, sociability, and energy." (Gladwell)

Traits common to Connectors are energy, a willingness to take chances, as well as an insistence that connecting is different from networking. Where networking is often regarded as a means to an end, connecting is driven by a genuine interest in other people and the appeal of engagement to better support and assist others.

This ability to influence and connect people must be balanced with the ability to get things done. A sociable "big idea" person who has trouble executing will not serve you well in this role. The champion must also emphasize focus, accomplishing results, and accountability.

My Own "Mentor Champion" Qualities

I am the program champion of the Executive Mentor Program at UWF and was recruited by Dr. Ed Ranelli, dean emeritus for the UWF College of Business, whose ideas about a champion are included farther below. As you seek a program champion, it may help to know a little more about me and why I am suited for this kind of work.

Before entering academia, I enjoyed a 20-year career as a marketing executive with Gannett Co., Inc. and later as vice president and chief marketing officer with a large regional health system. During those years, I made hundreds of connections with community business leaders. So, when needing to approach business leaders to become mentors, my phone contact database was full of skilled people to call upon. Many were, and still are, close friends.

Assessment tools such as the DISC assessment and the Myers–Briggs Type Indicator (MBTI) indicate behavioral style preferences and how people perceive the world and make decisions. Let me share with you the elements of my personality "type" from these two tools as a way to articulate characteristics to look for in a program champion.

My DISC report indicates a strong leaning toward two areas: Influence and Dominance. People who score high in Influence emphasize influencing or persuading others, openness, and relationships. They show enthusiasm, are optimistic, and like to collaborate. Scoring high in Dominance indicates a person who emphasizes accomplishing results, the bottom line, and is confident. They see the big picture, accept challenges, and get straight to the point.

In Myers-Briggs speak, I am an ENTJ, which stands for Extraverted, iNtuitive, Thinking, Judging within their 16 personality types. A person with this combination of preferences has qualities of enthusiasm, vision, objectivity, and accountability. ENTJs are efficient, energetic, self-confident, strong-willed, strategic thinkers, charismatic, and inspiring. If there is anything people with my personality type love, it's a good challenge, big or small. That's because we think that given enough time and resources, we can achieve any goal.

Denise Ivey, a past boss at Gannett, used to tell me that she appreciated my ability to think strategically and embrace a long-term focus while executing each step of our plans with determination and precision—a characteristic typical of ENTJs. I've also been called tenacious, pushing toward goals with sheer willpower and pushing everyone else along with me (also an ENTJ characteristic).

"When in charge of an organization, whether in the military, business, education, or government, ENTJs desire and have the ability to visualize where the organization is going, and they seem unusually able to communicate that vision to others," writes David Keirsey in *Please Understand Me II*. (Keirsey)

In full transparency, ENTJs such as myself have weaknesses that might concern a hiring manager. We can be seen as stubborn and dominant (sometimes capable of digging in our heels), intolerant ("It's my way or the highway"), and impatient (some people need more time to think than others, which can frustrate an ENTJ). But as you can also see, ENTJs have the drive and determination to set goals and bring plans to fruition, and these are qualities that will make your program champion successful.

At Navy Federal Credit Union, the talent development team manages their sizeable mentorship program. To be on the team, individuals must have an unrelenting commitment to development and unwavering customer focus. When selecting the program leader, Navy Federal Credit Union's Thomas Greek says, "Find someone who is committed to development and making the voice of the customer their mission. These are critical skills. They should understand the importance of a mentorship relationship and be a cultural champion."

Finding the Right Person to Lead Your Program

First, to give you an outside perspective on what to look for when hiring your champion, here is what Dr. Ranelli said you should look for in a person who can fill this role. A few descriptors listed relate to the higher education field, but everything else is relevant to the business world.

Your program champion:

- Must have a passion for giving back and passing on wisdom to the next generation
- Should be an affable, pleasant personality who loves being around people
- Must have a broad, diverse network and be well-liked—and respected—among community leaders, faculty, and professional leaders

- Should be smart, strategic, and well organized
- Must be energetic with a deep desire to make a difference in people's lives and careers
- Should have both academic and business experience and credentials
- Must be comfortable networking and knowledgeable about working in the academic world and the business world
- Must want to make an enduring difference and build — not simply maintain the status quo
- Must have a long-term perspective and not be a short-termer

✓ Success Secret: Ensure Leadership Support

The champion must also be someone who has the full, unwavering support of the top leader (CEO, dean) who shares a passion for giving back and preparing people for successful careers and lives, said Dr. Ranelli. If you want to succeed in developing people, you have to make it a top priority.

So we have established that your champion must be a connector who is confident, tenacious, and great with people, and who can easily see opportunities to bring together the mentors and mentees who will be good fits for each other. Think of the list of criteria offered above by Dr. Ranelli: Who in your organization matches this list?

The sooner you can identify a person who is champion material (or at least come up with a few possible candidates to consider), you will be well on your way to making your vision of a mentor program a reality.

In my experience, the best candidate to lead the mentoring program is often quite apparent. However, if you need help finding and appointing the champion, you could ask senior leaders to name a few candidates and interview them. I would not put out a call to interested parties, because you could get people whose personal characteristics are not suited for the role, and you wouldn't want to discourage employees or make them feel bad.

It may take a little while to find and appoint your program champion. That's okay. Take your time and make sure you get the right person for the job. When you get this part right, you'll save yourself a lot of frustration later. In the next chapter, we will start taking a look at the metrics you can use to measure your program's success.

Gladwell, Malcolm. The Tipping Point: How Little Things Can Make a Big Difference. Back Bay Books, 2002.
Keirsey, David. Please Understand Me II: Temperament, Character, Intelligence. Prometheus Nemesis, 2006.

CHAPTER 10

Step 3: Set Goals and Metrics

As we discussed earlier, it's important to get senior leaders on board with your mentoring program from the start. This means making the business case for why it is needed. Identifying the objectives up front will help align your mentoring program outcomes with your business objectives, illustrating to senior leaders why mentoring should be a priority.

You may have identified most of your program goals when you considered your "why." We offered a few ideas in Step 1. But now it's time for the program manager and leadership team to sit down and really focus on them. Throughout this process, remember that your program can't be everything to everyone. Keep it simple and targeted.

It's time to ask yourself: What is the opportunity you visualize for:

- You and your organization?
- Mentors?
- Mentees?

It's time to move beyond generalities! (A goal without numbers attached is really just a wish.)

Translate Your Mentoring Vision into SMART Objectives

Your program objectives provide direction to participating mentors and mentees, while key performance indicators help organizational leaders understand why they should support the program. As you determine your program's goals and needs, think about what metrics you will use to measure movement toward your business goals, using the SMART method: Specific, Measurable, Attainable, Relevant, and Time-bound metrics. In addition to these characteristics, useful mentoring metrics are:

- **Comparative.** Compare numbers across time periods to define movement toward business goals. "Increase top-employee retention by 10 percent from last year."
- **Understandable.** Show the numbers you are tracking to outsiders, possibly a board of directors, and see if they quickly grasp the needle you are trying to move. If they can, your metrics are understandable. If people can't talk about it and discuss it, it's much harder to change things significantly.
- **Expressed in a ratio or rate.** Indicate the relative sizes of two or more numbers. For example, 30 percent of employees are "very satisfied" with current career advancement opportunities available to them in our company; the other 70 percent *aren't* very satisfied.
- **Behavior-changing.** Ask yourself what you will do if those numbers go up, down, or stay the same. What will you do differently, as the program champion, based on the results of these metrics? If you don't know, look for better metrics to track. For instance, you could decide to measure the page-views of your mentor program website. But what will you change about the program or do differently if the numbers go up? Or down? Or stay the same? My guess is not much since page-views are not relevant to your program's achieving its goals for your mentees.

A better metric to track would be the number of people who express interest in participating in your program. If the number is low, you could pursue various solutions: a focus on program visibility and recruiting, for instance. This is your starting point for a future of tracking and reporting meaningful progress. Think it through carefully and make sure the program goals make sense for what your organization wants to achieve. We will discuss the tracking and reporting process in more detail later.

For right now, tie these metrics to both business goals for your company and professional development goals for your employees. For instance, Cox Communications measures the effectiveness of their executive mentoring program through promotion and retention rates.

Look back at the Define Your "Why" chapter and you'll see we mentioned a few broad reasons to establish a mentoring program. Metrics for some of these examples might be:

- Five senior leaders will have written a succession plan by the end of 18 months.
- Double the number of women in C-suite from two to four in 18 months.
- Reduce the number of key employees who leave by 50 percent. (Of course, now you must also define key employees—you can see why this step is important!)

UWF
CASE STUDY

How UWF Set Goals and Metrics for Our Mentoring Program

The Problem: As you will recall from Step 1, the UWF "why" is to help students improve their workforce readiness, which requires a combination of social, personal, and applied cognitive skills. The end result is to help students obtain and succeed in professional positions in their fields after graduation.

The Solution: The College of Business created the Executive Mentor Program. It is a high-impact practice (HIP). HIPs are effective for student learning, engagement, and career preparation. The program, started in 2012, pairs business executives one-on-one with juniors, seniors, and graduate students for an academic year or more. The mentees and mentors meet at least one to two hours a month to focus on the development of necessary skills. Once acquired, we put these skills into practice with monthly programs that include meet-and-greet networking events, lectures, and training workshops that focus on such topics as leadership skills.

The Business Goal: The goal/need of the university and the mentors (business executives in our community) was the same:

- **Primary Goal:** Lagging indicator: 100 percent of college students who want to will gain jobs in their fields upon graduation. (We know we can't control the lagging indicator, but it is our end goal.)

- **Primary Need:** Leading indicator: Ensure that our college students are better prepared to enter the workforce. (We can impact the leading indicator, and it is what drives the lagging indicator and helps us achieve the end goal.)

The Professional Development Goal: For the college student mentees:

- **Primary Goal:** Lagging indicator: 100 percent of the students who want to will gain jobs in their fields upon graduation.

- **Primary Need:** Leading indicator: Improve the students' intangible "human skills," defined as professionalism, teamwork, leadership skills, self-confidence, knowledge of the business community, a better understanding of his/her strengths and weaknesses, verbal and written communication skills, critical thinking skills, and networking skills.

Our Leading Indicator Key Metrics: We created a list of learning objectives, built a survey around them, and then evaluated the outcomes. Our goals were that as a result of participating in the Executive Mentor Program, 70 percent of mentees would show improvement in each of the following areas:

- Gains a better understanding of professionalism
- Advances their understanding of teamwork
- Develops his/her leadership skills
- Gains more self-confidence
- Expands his/her knowledge of the business community
- Better understands his/her strengths and weaknesses
- Improves his/her verbal communication skills
- Improves his/her written communication skills
- Increases his/her critical thinking skills
- And is more prepared to enter the workforce

We had two additional critical program metrics. One, that 70 percent of participants were highly satisfied, indicating they had a positive experience. Two, that 70 percent of participants would be willing to recommend the program to a friend or colleague, our net promoter score.

In the very first year, UWF blew those goals out of the water. So, every year, we keep working to improve year-over-year. In Chapter 14: Step 7: Measure to Improve, we'll take a look at the most current results broken down by survey questions. Suffice it to say that we're over the 90 percent mark with those two critical metrics and well above the desired 70 percent mark in almost every area.

One caveat: Don't measure success on numerical data alone. When making a business case for your mentor program, include a combination of numerical data and personal stories. It is important not to rely on just the numbers. Numbers alone can fall short in measuring the most essential part of any mentoring program: people. Stories help you describe and measure the "unmeasurable." And, people are not always inspired by numbers. People are inspired by great stories. We'll provide you with the best practices for this later.

✓ Success Secret: Focus Mentoring Efforts on Intangible "Human Skills"

You may have noticed that the University of West Florida's Executive Mentor Program is very much linked to the development of intangible "human skills" (see the list on the following page). This is by design! People are reaching out for the kinds of skills that will serve them well in the future. While "hard skills" are focused on the specific knowledge, tasks, and abilities required for success in a job, the intangible "soft skills" are becoming more and more desired.

For example, more in-demand online courses feature skills such as emotional intelligence and critical thinking. In addition, research shows that professional workers are seeking ways to learn soft skills at a higher rate than ever. This is excellent news for forward-thinking CEOs considering a formal mentoring program since intangible skill development is where mentoring shines. And these are permanent skills. No matter how the world changes, people need these intangible "human skills" to be successful in their careers and lives.

Unlike training on computer software packages, data analytics, UX design, or blockchain, training on the intangible skills that make for great leadership and spark personal development tend to be longer-term in nature. Still, they have excellent short-term benefits: employee engagement, morale, and interest in the broader organization, to name just a few. A friend of mine has done exercises to compare tangible and intangible skills, particularly in why projects fail or succeed. He found that most of the time it's due to intangible skills advancing a mission. What organizations need are more leaders who get things done at intangible AND tangible levels.

Intangible "Human Skills":

- Professionalism
- Communication
- Trust
- Motivation
- Inspiration
- Leadership
- Critical thinking
- Self-confidence
- Teamwork
- Knowledge of the business community
- Self-awareness (understanding personal strengths and weaknesses)
- Verbal and written communication skills
- Networking skills
- Character
- Values
- Empathy
- Capacity for respect

Once you have established the metrics you will use to indicate your mentoring program's success, it will be time to start making it a reality through…you guessed it, more planning. But remember, the more planning you do, the more prepared you will be when it's time to launch your mentoring program. In the following chapter, we will dive into the nuts and bolts of building your program, including securing organizational support, figuring out the financial aspects, and identifying needed training materials, and more.

"The Labor Market for Recent College Graduates." Federal Reserve Bank of New York, 2021.

CHAPTER 11

Step 4: Build Your Program

Now that you are 100 percent onboard with the need to launch a mentoring program, you likely want it done—yesterday! You are ready to jump into starting the program now, right? But you can't do that just yet. First, you need a plan of action—the road map or blueprint that will guide you through the process.

You might be wondering, *Why take the time to "design" a program structure? Why not just dive in and build it as we go?*

Here's why: The blueprint provides the objective, scope, clear steps, resources required, and targets, measurements, and analysis for your mentoring program. This not-to-be-missed step contains the "hard" plan elements of structure, systems, and support. Not only that, it should also include less tangible elements such as shared values, style, and the core competencies or skills of the employees who will implement the program.

Designing the architecture of your program for sustainable impact is essential. As French writer Antoine de Saint-Exupéry said, "A goal without a plan is just a wish."(Chernev)

Just to give you some perspective, there will be plenty of action steps to take once all of your planning is complete. Broadly speaking, when you set up your mentoring program, you will have a recruitment phase, training time, a mentoring phase, and an end phase (see "Set Clear Checkpoints" in Step 6). During the mentoring phase, you will need to have formal and informal ways to check in with the mentors and mentees to ensure things are going smoothly. As you read further, you may find other ideas to include in your program—networking events, a formal thank-you program, etc.

For now, though, we will cover some of the granular steps involved in designing and building your program. Remember that a well-thought-out plan means less trial and error, fewer mistakes, and fewer course corrections. So take your time and think carefully about each step below.

Present a Clear Business Case to Stakeholders

To create a thriving mentoring program, you need to get buy-in, approval, and support from your organization's stakeholders. It's time to make your case. This means you need to clearly state the program's business objectives, aligning your intentions with the organization's strategic goals. Stakeholders could be your boss or the CEO. Or, if *you* are the CEO, they could include your board of directors and your senior management team. In higher education, they could be the dean or the university president.

Regardless, to win over stakeholders, you will want to take a heart-and-mind approach in your presentation. Include a blend of metrics and ROI along with the emotional convincers of relatable stories or a case study or two.

UWF
CASE STUDY

Making the Business Case

One of my research focus areas is workforce readiness and mentoring. Before launching our program at UWF, we made a clear business case to the College of Business Dean's Office and local business executives, using national research and local anecdotal information. We shared data that showed that college students' workforce readiness (meaning that graduates have a good combination of social, personal, and applied cognitive skills) fell short of employer requirements nationally. This had negatively impacted new graduates' ability to obtain and succeed in professional positions in their fields, with 60 percent or less getting jobs in their fields after graduation. ("The Labor Market for Recent College Graduates") We also shared individual stories and comments from area business leaders expressing the same concerns locally.

Together, our deans and business community rallied around this news, with everyone jumping on board to support the mentoring program to solve the problem.

Since 2012, I continue to gather and analyze data annually to evaluate our mentoring program's effectiveness and share the findings with key stakeholders. Our stakeholders appreciate knowing 1) the program is working and their efforts are not wasted, and 2) that we care enough to strive for continuous improvement in the program. As a result, we continue to have, even when budgets are lean, strong support of time and money invested in the mentoring program.

Ensure Organizational Support for the Program

Mentoring programs will be most successful with support from high places. (And depending upon your position in the organization, that might include you!) If you are the CEO, are you fully committed to this investment? If you are at a college, do you have leadership support? If you are in HR, do you have senior leadership behind you?

By support, I mean a willingness to sign off on the program financially, divert people and resources from other initiatives if needed, and talk up the mentoring program and encourage people to participate. Visible support from top leadership is priceless.

As mentioned in Step 1, there are often several layers of stakeholders. These include upper management who finance the endeavor, a champion of the initiative, and those who will help launch the program. There must be a high level of support from each of these groups. And before you begin, you must know you have the leadership backing necessary to be successful.

Unfortunately, many universities lack staffing capacity or resources to implement mentoring programs, which are labor-intensive for faculty and administrators. This is especially true considering programs must have defined student learning outcomes that are measured and evaluated if they are to be effective. There are no easy solutions. Using appropriate grant funding, reallocating resources from lower-impact initiatives, and pursuing sponsorships are a few ways to address minimal people resources.

UWF
CASE STUDY

Our "Support" Is Expressed in Hours

At the University of West Florida, our program has the full support of the university president and the college dean. The team includes:

- one faculty/program leader—20 hours per week

- one administrative employee—40 hours per week

- and, often, two student workers—15 hours per week (up to 30 hours total)

We make sure to allow enough hours to facilitate the program properly. This can sometimes mean that if there is something we feel we should add to our program, such as more training, we consider what we will spend less time on (for example, we might hold fewer events during the year). It's a conscious and deliberate decision.

Ensuring leadership support is just as essential at a large, worldwide organization such as Navy Federal Credit Union (if not more so).

"Senior leadership support is critical because it validates and reiterates the importance of talent development as part of the culture," says Navy Federal's Thomas Greek. "This support also encourages other leaders throughout the organization to volunteer their time as mentors. It encourages their team members to participate in the program."

Define the Resource Investment

Defining the resource investment needed for your program is a step you'll want to do in tandem with making a case for the program to your stakeholders. To gain stakeholder buy-in and support, they need to know why the program is necessary and its cost. Based on the size and scope of the mentoring program you plan to create, you'll need to determine the people and financial resources needed to achieve your goals and objectives. Your organization may need one, more, or all of the following budget items:

- Payroll
- Office space, equipment, supplies
- Website design and maintenance
- Brochures and forms
- Training materials; cost of a trainer
- Marketing and communication materials
- Social media expense (possible internal transfer of staff time)
- Meeting/event expenses for meet-and-greet networking events, lectures, and training workshops
- Guest speaker expenses
- Technology platforms

In recognition of how powerful mentoring is, Cox Communications has invested in technology platforms to provide opportunities for mentors and mentees to connect. As Kia Painter says, "This affords the ability to facilitate matching faster and gives us insights about the connections so that we can begin to measure." (We'll talk more about these measurements in Chapter 14.)

Decisions You'll Need to Make to Create Great Learning Experiences

How well your employees engage with your mentoring program will determine how successful it will be. The biggest driver of this is whether the program is effectively meeting their needs. An important question to ask yourself ahead of time is, *What does success look like for our participants?* If your employees don't think that your program is beneficial, it will be challenging to get them to do that thing you want them to do in order to improve.

To answer this question, make sure you understand who the mentees are, their development needs, and their key motivations to participate. When designing your mentoring program, here are some of the decisions you'll have to make:

- How are mentors and mentees selected to participate? Is it by invitation only, or is it open so any employee can apply?
- What is the selection process? Will there be an application form? An interview? Both?
- Assuming you will have 1:1 mentoring, how long will the connection be in place? One year? Longer?
- Will there be any training of mentors? Mentees? If yes, what form(s) will that training take? Training offers the opportunity for engaging learning experiences. At our UWF orientation training sessions for mentors, for example, we take the opportunity to teach the mentors what is expected, which is standardized for everyone, and make it an in-person interactive session. They get to know the other new mentors and become acquainted with and learn from our veteran mentors. This informal meeting, usually during a working lunch, provides the opportunity to explain the leeway mentors are given for shaping their mentoring experiences and the few firm expectations that must be met.
- In addition to the 1:1 mentoring, will there be other components of the program? Will you host networking events? How will you provide recognition? What additional communication will you establish?
- How, and how often, will you evaluate the program?

I will discuss how to approach each of these questions as you go through the rest of this book.

Create Branded Program Resources

The main reason branding is essential for a mentoring program is for getting recognition and becoming known to the key stakeholders. Creating a name, logo, design, and color scheme that is easily identifiable as belonging to your program is valuable for many reasons. It helps identify your mentoring program, makes a memorable impression, and distinguishes it from other initiatives.

Branding can help you get people excited about being a part of the program, including your president and CEO, senior leaders, mentors, mentees, and the organization as a whole. And if done well, it can make your program visible and appealing to your external customers and potential employees as well. Branding will make your program feel "real" and be taken seriously.

Once you've developed your brand, how do you get the word out? Here are a few simple tips:

- Use the same color scheme, logo, look, and feel on everything—no need to be fancy, just consistent.
- Write down the key messages you want to communicate about your program and use them often.
- Design branded templates (to make your life easier) and create brand standards for your marketing materials.
- Create a website (or pages on your organization's website). Key components could include the program's mission, goals, and objectives; information about how to become a mentor or a mentee; and upcoming events. Once the program is operational, a website is a great place to show photos, videos, and participants' testimonials.
- Produce informational brochures and videos. These should be broad in scope so that you can share them with any stakeholder group who wants to learn about the program (senior leaders, potential mentors, potential mentees, and the public). Have branded business cards available to

distribute to anyone interested in the program, so they can easily follow up for more information if interested.

- Establish well-branded visibility at in-person meetings and events with banners, tablecloths, signage, and pens.

Promoting your mentoring program doesn't stop after it gets started. You should frequently remind mentors and mentees, as well as new prospects, what mentoring can do for them—and your branding materials will be an ongoing reminder.

✕ Potential Pitfall: Low Participation in Your Mentoring Program

The fear of "what if no one participates" haunts any mentoring program leader. Companies or colleges that launch and then drop a mentoring program are gravely disappointed and miss a golden opportunity. Enthusiasm doesn't always lead to participation. Like any other initiative, effective marketing is essential.

Developing a great marketing plan for the mentoring program can make a huge difference. Whether through emails and flyers or phone calls and meetings, make sure your potential participants understand the value to them.

Once you have your branding ready, you can create your recruiting materials.

Create Recruitment Processes and Materials

Next up, it's time to establish or create the processes or materials for your mentoring program. Some of these will be public-facing as they are aimed at attracting program participants, while other materials are for internal use. As you develop your materials, keep in mind that your mentoring program can help shape the overall culture you want to create within your company. Be intentional with the words and images you choose—they're more powerful than you may realize in terms of setting expectations and driving outcomes.

This portion of your planning could include:

- Establishing the process for applying to the program. Be sure to make it easy for mentors and mentees alike to sign up.
- Creating applications. Create a matching application (one for mentors and one for mentees) that prompts both parties to share who and what they are looking for in a mentoring relationship.
- Setting up a user-profile database with rich data such as gender, college, interests, industry, job function, contact information.
- Creating promotional flyers to spread the word about the program.
- Crafting scripts for recruitment phone calls and emails.
- Setting agendas for informational meetings with prospective mentors and mentees.
- Establishing a process and list of questions for vetting potential mentors and mentees during one-on-one interviews with the program manager.
- Creating contract forms (to be signed). These contracts provide a simple framework for the mentors/mentees to follow. For example, it might state that pairs should meet once per month for a year.

Create Training Materials

Being a good mentor or mentee is a learned skill. Therefore, it is important to create materials aimed at preparing mentors (and mentees) for their upcoming roles. Items could include:

- New participant (mentor and mentee) orientation onboarding materials. Include all the facts, dates, deadlines, and contact information a participant may need.
- Orientation PowerPoint. Create a presentation that can be used to train new mentors and mentees before they begin the program.
- Orientation video to share with new participants. It can include past participants, both mentors and mentees, talking about the value of the program to them.
- Commitment forms. It's a good idea to have a commitment form for participants to sign, stating they understand the expectations. It helps reinforce the importance of the program.
- Sample "icebreaker" questions. (Hint: See Chapter 3 in Bert's part of the book.)
- Talking points/tip sheets/learning guides for both mentees and mentors. Here, you might revisit Bert's part of the book. He addresses all sorts of helpful topics around how to be a great mentor, characteristics of a successful mentee, how to assess the mentee (based on the "Eight Great Social Tells"), and more. You can pull from Bert's content to create helpful materials, or you can simply hand mentors a copy of the book so that they might develop their own.
- Self-assessment learning for mentees to share with mentors (for example, the MBTI test and/or DISC assessment).

Mentoring Benefits of Self-Assessment Tools Such as MBTI and DISC

Assessment tools provide valuable in-depth information about one's behavioral characteristics, value to the organization, ideal environment, perceptions when under stress, and adaptations to be more successful. The results reveal how the individual prefers to be managed, motivated, and communicated with.

"Self-awareness and behavior change is critical to the development of effective leaders," says executive mentor

Carol Carlan, founder and CEO of Carlan Consulting, LLC, a company dedicated to assisting individuals to become the best leaders. She adds, "Scientifically based and proven assessments bring objective, accurate, and actionable information to the coaching and mentoring process."

One such proven assessment is the DISC, which stands for Dominance, Influence, Steadiness, and Compliance. Another tool is MBTI, which stands for Myers-Briggs Type Indicator. This tool identifies and describes 16 distinctive personality types that result from interactions among individual preferences.

When a mentee shares their self-assessment findings with their mentor, it provides a tool for the mentor to use to help their mentee learn how to leverage their strengths, uncover blind spots, and work on areas that may be limiting them.

Be sure to incorporate learning opportunities, whether through guest speakers or reading materials, about important topics to your program. For instance, at the UWF College of Business, we believe understanding business ethics helps our graduates reason, dialogue, and act on ethical matters. To that end, we bring in guest speakers to talk to our participants—both mentors and mentees—about using good judgment and making ethical decisions in the workplace. The speakers reinforce the courage required to make not just the legal decisions, but the right ones.

Additionally, be prepared to provide your mentors and mentees recommended reading lists, books, podcasts, online learning, etc. These can be books on the industry you are in or the role the mentee is aspiring to move into. Leadership books are always good reading for future leaders.

Discussion Topics/Tips to Include in Training Materials and Orientations for Mentees:

- Don't treat the mentoring relationship like a transaction. The relationship is not about what a mentee can "get" from the mentor. Instead it should be about establishing a deep connection to gain an understanding of career paths, goals, and interests.

- Show up prepared with questions.
- Treat meetings like a meeting with the boss. Set the agenda ahead of time and be proactive about the content of the meeting so that mentors can be prepared with pertinent thoughts, examples, and a sense of how they can help. Mentees should focus on one topic for each meeting and bring questions they have on that topic.
- If you don't share, your mentor cannot help and may become frustrated.
- Choose a challenge and say: "I'm going to tackle this problem. Here's what I'm considering doing and why. How does that sound to you?" That way, mentors can help ensure it is realistic. Don't simply ask the mentor what they would do. Have a solution ready and get their feedback.
- Don't boil the ocean in every meeting. One thing that can happen during mentorship meetings is that there can be far too much to discuss. Few mentees have only one major challenge or problem on their plate. It can be tempting to try to discuss everything that's going on. This will limit how deep your conversation can go on the issues that matter most. If you have a big challenge, try to break it down into parts to discuss over several meetings. This could be the agenda for your first mentee/mentor meeting: how to break your complex goals into manageable parts.

Develop Ongoing Communication Channels

There are many individuals you must communicate with throughout your program. The goal is to communicate effectively and efficiently, but not constantly—and without taking time away from getting other work done. (This can be a tough balance to strike!) Often, program managers choose to communicate in a way that works best *for them*; however, this may not necessarily work best for the mentors and mentees. Everyone absorbs information differently. To engage everyone, it's best to communicate in several different ways.

Possible communications could include:

- E-newsletters. Send these out monthly. You can use them to share upcoming events and best practices, feature a mentor or mentee, etc.
- Social media promotions. Use them, with hashtags, to gain visibility and interest and promote upcoming events or meetings.
- Closed LinkedIn group. Give your mentors and mentees a professional way to connect with one another.
- Website. This should include everything important about your program that anyone would want to know. As mentioned earlier, key components could include: the mission, goals, and objectives of the program; information about how to become a mentor or a mentee; and upcoming events. Once the program is operational, a website is a great place to show photos, videos, and testimonials of participants.

✓ Success Secret: Technology Alone Does Not Lead to Mentoring Outcomes—Don't Count on It to Do the Work for You

If all we needed was a platform, LinkedIn would have solved the challenges of mentorship years ago. An over-reliance on electronic tools can result in low engagement, so it's important to ensure there is also personal interaction for meaningful impact, even if that face-to-face interaction occurs via technology such as video conferencing.

Plan Professional Development Activities and Engagement Opportunities

Aside from regular mentor and mentee meetings, start thinking about and planning additional ways for participants to connect and learn. These could include:

- **Meet-and-greet networking events.** This type of event is a must-have. It enables the mentors and mentees in the program to get to know one another in an informal business setting. It's also an effective way to expand and build connections and cultivate professional relationships. Through conversations at these events, rising-star mentees can learn how to navigate a large organization, identify new career options, and create natural opportunities to help others. Savvy mentors can find talent for open roles on their team.
- **Guest speaker lectures.** At UWF, as at other universities, the relationship between academia and the professional world is vital. This is evidenced by the many business leaders who come to campus as guest speakers. Lectures provide an opportunity for students and our business executive mentors to learn from prominent leaders. Speakers can bring complex issues to life in a way a textbook can't. Listening to a great guest speaker, such as Bert, helps people broaden their knowledge in an exciting, interactive way.
- **Hands-on workshops.** Workshops bring the same value as guest speaker lectures, with the added value of participants' being able to apply what they learned and have conversations about it.
- **Conferences.** By attending a conference (whether in person or virtually), mentors and mentees expand their professional and personal development and acquire insightful information. Everyone gains fresh perspective

and has the opportunity to network, learn something new, and, hopefully, come away with new ideas.

- **Recognition ceremonies.** These make people feel that what they accomplished is valued. They show approval and gratitude for each person's efforts, both mentors and mentees. Recognition motivates people. A ceremony is also a chance for celebration and reflection. Gathering and sharing experiences is a powerful means of encouragement. Also, even for the program manager, having a sense of accomplishment drives improvement.

Embrace Modern Adult Learner Preferences

Mentoring is helping people learn and grow to be their best. In this book, we're focused on adult learners, whether they are college students or are professionals in the workforce. So, you should know a bit about them.

Research shows the modern adult learner is busy, savvy, and hungry to learn. And, it isn't a secret that today if an organization isn't enabling workers to develop professionally, they'll leave. According to LinkedIn's 2019 Workplace Learning Report, 94 percent of employees would stay at a company if it invested in their career development. ("Workplace Learning Report")

While the implementation of a mentoring program is an excellent career development opportunity, the mentoring experience has to be valuable and relevant to engage both mentors and mentees. Today's learners want personalized, timely, quality guidance, and relevance is king. They prefer when they can integrate their learning/mentoring into work or school, making knowledge-sharing and collaboration more relevant and efficient.

While adult learners today, as you would expect, are interested in promotions and salary increases, they are also eager to do their jobs well and to improve themselves personally. The learning derived from mentoring brings pleasure, a sense of worth, and has value in itself.

So what are the fundamental principles? Adult learners:

- Are self-directed
- Come to training with a lifetime of existing experience, knowledge, and opinions
- Are goal-oriented
- Want relevant training
- Learn when they see "what's in it for them"
- Want to be and feel respected

Therefore, when training:

- Be personal.
- Respect your audience.
- Meet clear goals.
- Avoid box-ticking exercises.
- Respect time.
- Produce insightful, useful learning experiences.

When creating your materials, keep the following points in mind:

- Always focus on what your participants need, not on what's easy for your program staff.
- Include as much hands-on practice as possible; people learn by doing.
- Break your meetings into small one- or two-hour meetings that are easier to take in and understand than marathon sessions.
- Try to integrate storytelling and scenarios into examples.
- Develop the expectations: "The best mentoring relationships have clearly defined rules of engagement. That means participants agree to a realistic schedule and, as much as possible, stick to an agenda when they meet."

—Ian Altman in *Forbes* (Altman)

As you can see, building a mentoring program is a huge amount of work and a significant commitment. After reading this chapter, you might be thinking, *I'm not sure we can really swing this right now.* If so, you can always start with a pilot program. Start with a few enthusiastic mentors and mentees, solicit feedback on their experiences, and make changes. Then gradually roll out a larger program incorporating that feedback, along with executive buy-in and commitments from mentors to serve. To harness the power of a mentoring program, you need competent people to guide it, coordinate it, and communicate its activities.

Just because you build it, that doesn't mean they will come. No matter how well built the program is or how excited you are to get it started, if you don't promote it effectively and don't recruit and train the participants well, your program will struggle. You must have a plan to attract and retain participants to build your voluntary army. That is what we'll discuss in the next chapter.

"The Labor Market for Recent College Graduates." Federal Reserve Bank of New York, 2021.
"Workplace Learning Report." 3rd ed., 2019, p. 38. general editor, LinkedIn.
Altman, Ian. "The Dos and Don'ts of Mentoring." 2017.
Chernev, Alexander. *The Marketing Plan Handbook.* 6th ed., Cerebellum Press, 2020.

CHAPTER 12

Step 5: Recruit and Connect

"While I made my living as a coach, I have lived my life to be a mentor—and to be mentored—constantly," wrote legendary basketball coach John Wooden in the book he coauthored with Don Yaeger, *A Game Plan for Life: The Power of Mentoring*. Coach Wooden called mentoring one of the most important things he did in his life. (Wooden and Yaeger)

This chapter is all about the Three Ms: mentors, mentees, and matching. Keep Coach Wooden's words in mind as you go about recruiting mentors and mentees and matching them—the topics we will cover in this section. This is a critical chapter! Your success here may turn out to be a turning point in the lives of the mentees you recruit.

All three aspects are equally important. According to Wendy Murphy, PhD, a mentoring expert and coauthor of *Strategic Relationships at Work* (Murphy and Kram), people who have a mentor:

- Are more likely to be promoted faster
- Get more opportunities to begin with

- Earn higher salaries
- Actually like their jobs more

"That's the secret," she says. "Mentoring is a mutual relationship, so there are benefits in both directions. Oftentimes people who mentor more are more satisfied at their work as well as they've become known as developing others.

"Furthermore, the organization develops," she adds. "It creates what's called the 'developmental culture,' where people are helping one another navigate their careers." (Murphy)

Recruit, Train, and Retain Your Volunteer Army

Let's begin with mentor recruiting. We need to attract, screen, and engage great mentors. We must help them understand the value of participating. And we must train them to be highly effective.

All of this starts with great communication. As with any communication, your messages must be clear and compelling. Don't just promote the features of the program; communicate the benefits. Spell out what mentors and mentees have to gain on both personal and professional levels.

For some, this might be the first time they have participated in a mentoring program, so you convince them that taking part is a valuable use of their time and energy. And as we've discussed before, it's essential to communicate to your company's leadership team the strategic value of the program to the organization.

Set Effective Expectations for Mentors and Mentees

You don't want someone to apply for the program thinking one thing, only to be disappointed to find out the reality is something completely different. Therefore, it's important to:

- Clearly articulate the mission, vision, and goals of the program during recruitment.
- Spell out the time commitment for mentors and mentees. They are volunteering their time and should know what the minimum expectation is. Most mentors volunteer on a combination of "company" time and their personal "after-hours" unpaid time.
- As Bert mentioned, the personal relationship between mentor and mentee may continue for a lifetime, but for program purposes, you must define the length of their "official" pairing. Is it one year? Two? It's good to have a defined end to the commitment, even if you allow participants to re-up for an additional year. (Tip: Six months or less is not enough time to build rapport, establish trust, set personal goals, and make a long-term difference. In my experience, a 12-month official mentoring relationship works well, and can be renewed for another term when appropriate.)
- Ensure that mentees know there will be some work for them to do. It's not all listening to mentors share sage advice over coffee!
- Require applicants to make a real commitment to the relationship. You don't want to force it and make people sign in blood; nonetheless, make it serious. Have them sign a short one-page contract stating they will make the program a priority and honor their commitments to the program and one another. There is a difference between interest and commitment. Again, it has to be *their* decision to commit, not the organization's.

"Unless commitment is made, there are only promises and hopes, but no plans."

—Peter F. Drucker (Drucker)

Define Mentor Qualifications

The initial step is to determine the requirements of your ideal mentor. For example, do you want only people who have been in a leadership position within your company for five years or more? A cross-section of people from different departments across your organization? People with specific skill sets? An array of diverse backgrounds, ethnicities, etc.?

Of course the right attitude is important, too. As Mary Abbajay writes in *Forbes* (Abbajay), "A good mentor needs to be more than just a successful individual. A good mentor must have the disposition and desire to develop other people. It requires a willingness to reflect on and share one's own experiences, including one's failures." The program champion can determine whether a potential mentor has this quality by talking and spending time with them in an introductory interview.

UWF
CASE STUDY

What We Look for in a Mentor

In our Executive Mentor Program, we look for candidates with the following qualifications:

- Ten or more years of business experience at an executive level, such as owner, president, CEO, vice president, or partner, in northwest Florida

- A reputation for having strong business ethics and integrity (you can glean insight into this through references and interviews)

- A network of friends, colleagues, and coworkers who can be called on as resources to assist the student

And then, if someone meets these requirements, I (as program champion) also assess whether or not he or she has the five characteristics of a successful mentor that Bert explained earlier:

1. A sincere desire to reciprocate, to give back to the next generation of emerging leaders

2. A sincere interest in the mentee

3. A track record of demonstrated success

4. Knowledge, interest, or expertise in the mentee's specific area of interest

5. Peer respect

(As a reminder, see Chapter 1.)

Jodi Bell, regional vice president of sales for LOCALiQ/Gannett, is a great example. The way she talks about being an executive mentor in our program reveals her sincere interest in her mentees: "I see this as part of my legacy. The contribution of time that I make to each of these students will impact them for the rest of their lives, and I take that very seriously, and it's rewarding to me. All five [mentees] have been very different, and I count myself lucky to be on their personal board of directors. I believe that it is our responsibility as leaders to develop the next generation, and I take very seriously the concept of being able to inspire them to dream more, to learn more, to do more, and to become more."

Define the Mentor's Role

In the first half of this book, Bert details how to define the mentor's role and how mentors should interact during meetings with their mentees. To add to that, in a *Harvard Business Review* article (Tjan), Anthony Tjan, an entrepreneur and venture investor, highlights erroneous assumptions potential mentors may have and what a mentor's role should be:

"Too many mentors see mentoring as a training program focused around the acquisition of job skills," he writes. "Obviously, one element of mentorship involves mastering the necessary competencies for a given position. But the best leaders go beyond competency, focusing on helping to shape other people's character, values, self-awareness, empathy, and capacity for respect."

✗ Potential Pitfall: Mentors Shouldn't Try to Create "Mini-Mes"

Some mentors make the mistake of trying to fashion their mentees into mini versions of themselves. Should a mentor be a role model? Yes! The surest way to achieve success is to learn from the best. That doesn't mean, however, the mentee should copy everything about the mentor. Mentees need to keep a sense of self and follow their own path. Mentors should help mentees realize their goals, giving them the freedom to bring their own ideas to life.

"The delicate balance of mentoring someone is not creating them in your own image, but giving them the opportunity to create themselves."

—Steven Spielberg (Koifman)

UWF
CASE STUDY

Mentor Roles and Responsibilities

At UWF, volunteer mentors are executive-level business people who agree to communicate with students at least once per month through the academic school year.

We clearly articulate to our mentors that this is an opportunity for them to share their professional experience, knowledge, and skills with college students who are preparing to enter the business world. The mentor supports a student's personal and professional growth. The program provides a golden opportunity for executives to counsel and influence the next generation of business leaders.

Being a mentor provides personal satisfaction as well as the ability to increase the workforce readiness of future recruits. As mentors, executives help students clarify and achieve their personal and career goals through sharing support, along with offering friendship and professional advice.

Mentor Responsibilities

- Meet informally with the mentee at monthly meetings at the workplace or other business venues. The topics discussed at these meetings vary depending on the needs of the mentee. Everyone is different. Some mentees need help with self-confidence. Others need help knowing when to reign in their exuberance. There is no one cookie-cutter approach to these discussions. (Bert's part of the book sheds more light on this subject.)

- Be available to talk to the students through email or phone conversations as needed.

- Provide support and encouragement.

- Offer guidance and constructive criticism.

- Provide introductions and access to vital business circles.

- Demonstrate qualities successful business leaders possess.

- Help mentees clarify goals. These could be career goals, project goals, or life goals. Mentoring is about helping the mentee achieve their dreams.

Find Your Prospects and Vet Them

At this point, I suggest you develop a list of high-quality prospective mentors. I recommend you then have a well-known and respected leader in the organization (such as yourself or someone else the mentors know and respect) personally invite each prospective mentor to participate. This personal touch allows you to tell them about the program, explain the reasons they are a perfect candidate, briefly explain how the program works, and share the benefits of the program for the mentors, the mentees, and the organization.

Don't make participation in your mentoring program compulsory for your leaders. Bert and I agree: They might not be mentor material. They may not have the right temperament. And, mandating their involvement could make your leaders feel like you are just tacking one more thing onto their already-busy task list. This does not create buy-in or enthusiasm for the program. Instead, the leader is likely to simply go through the motions. Do ensure that people know this is an optional program that leadership looks upon favorably.

A component of your recruiting process needs to include vetting the mentors. At UWF, this involves a written screening and an interview with the program director to ensure they have relevant business experience and the characteristics needed. The beauty of this process is that influential, effective mentors stick around and bring in other effective mentors.

Recruit: Promote the Benefits to Potential Mentors

You have already determined the profile of your ideal mentor. Now you need to consider the needs of mentors. When potential mentors see the value to their own careers and businesses, participation rates go up. Consider both things they want as well as what they don't want. Figure out how you will reinforce the positive points and lessen the negative ones.

Lack of time is probably the biggest hurdle to overcome as you try to recruit busy executives to become program mentors. So be clear about how many hours every week or month you expect them to spend with their mentees. Our Executive Mentor Program is structured and designed with the limited schedule of a hardworking executive in mind. While our commitment is for a full year, the monthly time commitment required is typically no more than an hour of preparation and an hour to meet.

When I was speaking at a Rotary meeting, someone asked how I can recruit so many highly successful executives to be mentors in our program since they are so busy. The answer is that these mentors are skilled at time management. They make sure to carve out time for things they are passionate about. In fact, some executives consider "busy" to be a four-letter word. A friend, for example, told me she is working to remove that word from her vocabulary. When you say you're busy, the person you're directing it to could feel that they're not important—and she wants people she's talking with to know they are a priority to her.

Before you approach potential mentors, think through other objections you may hear and be ready with ways to overcome those objections.

But also, emphasize the gifts the mentors receive from their contribution. Cox Communications has seen the benefits to mentors, and they share them with future recruits. Kia Painter has this to say: "Mentoring has been a great avenue for creating connections among executives and emerging talent. For me personally, mentoring has served as a form of reflective practice for my own development as an executive, as I continue to think of ways to aid in my mentee's development."

UWF
CASE STUDY

How Our Mentors Benefit from the Program

While I realized from the start how much the student mentees would benefit from the mentorship program, what I soon realized—and continue to realize—is how much the mentors enjoy the program and the satisfaction they receive from participating. These quotes show how the program meets the intrinsic needs of our mentors:

- "I found that it keeps me sharp. If Morgan [his mentee] is coming by, I know that I have to be on my game, so it helps me. And, I have to practice what I preach. If I'm telling her these great business ideas, I feel like I actually have to implement those in my own business as well."

  —John Shaffer, franchise owner, State Farm

- "For me, it's important to give back...I find this is a very valuable opportunity to leverage my experience and pay it forward to those who are seeking that kind of knowledge and that kind of experience. You really receive the blessing on the other side."

  —Pam Hatt, vice president of marketing, Pen Air Federal Credit Union

- "It was really valuable for me to go through those experiences and those exercises with her because it renewed and restored my faith a little bit in the young people coming up who are going to be the next generation of professionals."

  —Amy Miller, deputy city administrator for administration & enterprises, City of Pensacola, FL

Perhaps Winston Churchill said it best: "We make a living by what we get; we make a life by what we give."

Define Mentee Qualifications

Up until now, we've been talking about mentors. Now you must determine the requirements of your ideal mentee. For example, do you want only people who have been with your organization for three years or more? A cross-section of various people from different departments across your organization? High performers with great potential? (With this last one, you will need to define what a high performer looks like!)

A large organization may need to set up a system to nominate mentees to a committee to keep the number of mentees manageable. Do not issue a "cattle call" for interested candidates. Likely, you won't be pleased with the results.

✓ Success Secret: 80/20 Rule— Focus Mentoring on the Top Performers

You've heard of the Pareto Principle (the 80/20 Rule), right? It is the observation that most things in life are not distributed evenly. Some contribute more than others. Consider this when determining whom to recruit as mentees for your program; you may be able to focus on your top 20 percent to achieve 80 percent of the new potential. In other words, invest your time in people who will give the greatest return.

Ask yourself, *Could the top 20 percent of my team be hungry to be exposed to new insights and perspectives while serving as a mentee to a more senior person in the organization? Or, might they be motivated by the opportunity to help mentor other up-and-comers within the organization? Would mentoring help catapult them to their next level professionally and personally?* If so, focus on including them in your mentoring program.

You can make decisions on allocating time, resources, and effort based on the 80/20 Rule. If you try to include too many people, you can spread yourself too thin. Caveat: Even though you might get the most bang for your buck in your mentoring program focused on your top 20 percent performers, that doesn't mean the other 80 percent of your team shouldn't be supported. They need appreciation and acknowledgment also. However, that can come from other initiatives that could serve them, and your company, more efficiently than a mentoring program. When you are trying to get the biggest bang for your buck, focusing on the critical 20 percent with your mentoring program is a time saver.

Once you have your mentoring program up and running smoothly and have the resources to invest in scaling it up, broaden its scope and include the oft-neglected "middle" performers. By this, I mean the middle 60 percent of employees who are your core performers. Imagine the benefits to your organization if your top performers are working at their peak, and you now also improve the attention, morale, and productivity of the 60 percent in the middle!

Most likely you'll want to develop a list of high-quality prospective mentees. Some companies develop this list through submissions from the management team. Other organizations note possible participation in a mentoring program during annual employee evaluations. Supervisors (and professors in the academic world) are good sources for gaining knowledge about possible mentees. I recommend you then have a well-known and respected leader in the organization (such as yourself) personally invite each prospective mentee to participate.

To effectively recruit mentees, ensure that people understand the value and benefits of participating. Offer training and reinforcement throughout the program while providing recognition for participation. It works.

UWF
CASE STUDY

What It Takes to Be a UWF Mentee

At UWF, to apply to be a mentee in our program, students must:

- Be full-time business students
- Be juniors, seniors, or graduate students
- Have a GPA of 3.0 or higher

As with selecting mentors, I interview students who have met these criteria to get a sense of whether or not they have the characteristics Bert mentioned are essential for mentees.

People sometimes ask why our program isn't open to first-year students and sophomores. It's another example of focusing on your end goal. Your program can't be everything to everybody. Our program's primary purpose is to prepare students for successful careers in business by integrating academic learning with real-world experiences to become a model for workforce readiness, embraced by the community. So we offer it to students who are nearing completion of their degree and actively preparing to enter the professional workforce.

Define What the Mentee's Role Is

In the first half of this book, Bert shares what makes a good mentee. For example, the mentee must truly want to be a mentee. They must have a real desire to learn, be open to advice, have a strong work ethic and the ability to follow through, and more. (As a reminder, see Chapter 2.)

Besides making sure mentees have the right qualifications, you'll need to decide what roles, specific to your program, the mentee must fulfill. For example, according to Kia Painter, mentees in the Cox Communications program are asked to do the following:

- Drive the relationship-planning meetings
- Commit to candor and confidentiality
- Own the learning experience, including:
  - Recap key takeaways from mentoring sessions
  - Share an action plan for development the mentor can offer advice on
  - Participate in a "job shadow" activity with the mentor

UWF
CASE STUDY

Mentee Responsibilities

- Take an active role in contacting the mentor and planning meeting times

- Commit to meeting monthly at the mentor's workplace or other business venues

- Be open, honest, and able to accept advice and constructive criticism in the spirit intended

- Have an agenda for their meetings to improve the content of conversations (What is it that they want to discuss with their mentor?)

Recruit: Promote the Benefits to Mentees

Once you have a good base of mentors, it's time to begin recruiting mentees. You created a list of criteria you're looking for in a mentee. Now, flip it around: What does the mentee want from your program? And, of course, what does the mentee *not* want? Figure out how you will reinforce the positive points and lessen the negative ones.

"The transportation and logistics industry is a male-dominated industry and has been for years. When I became a mentee in the UWF Executive Mentor Program, I was unsure who I was going to be paired with. However, once I was paired with Amy Miller, my life was forever changed. Amy, deputy city administrator for administration & enterprises, City of Pensacola, FL, gave me valuable insight into what it takes to be a successful businesswoman in transportation. Beyond the insight, I gained a role model and now a lifelong friend. Having a mentor helped me navigate the tricky waters of applying, interviewing, and generally building confidence in my abilities to tackle entry into the workforce after college successfully. After three years of working in transportation, I owe my success to Amy for her guidance and moral support."

—DaCotah Ledbetter, former UWF mentee, Chemours Dedicated Team Lead, Marten Transport, Ltd.

From experience, I've found that mentees, whether they are in college or are in the workplace, often want:

- Overall guidance on career development and to network with other people
- To learn more about a specific industry and career opportunities they should consider
- To gain knowledge about a specific area of the business
- To learn professional development skills that would benefit their career
- To increase their level of confidence in themselves and have someone they can bounce ideas off of

Lack of self-confidence is perhaps the biggest issue you might need to address when mentees consider applying to participate in a mentoring program. Get intentional about dispelling their fears and concerns. Be clear about the support mentees will receive from the program staff and that everyone realizes this is a learning experience. Mentees are not expected to have every answer—that's what the program and mentors are there to help them with.

Just be sure to emphasize to the mentees that they are considered perfect candidates for their potential. Explain how the program works and the benefit of the experience for them and the organization.

> UWF
> **CASE STUDY**

What a Mentor Brings to a Mentee's Life

At UWF, we continually communicate how having a mentor can help students:

- Clarify career goals
- Become ready for the workforce
- Increase business connections
- Heighten professional development
- Improve networking skills
- Enhance opportunities for future internships, jobs, and career success

We ask for feedback from our mentees regarding their needs and why they value their participation in the program. Then, we share quotes like these with potential mentees:

- "She helped strengthen my self-growth and professional development skills. Through our interactions, I was able to distinguish my core values and strive for a balance in all aspects of life, whether it be professional, academic, or personal. This phenomenal experience empowered me to maintain my ambitious and persevering characteristics and substantiated my career goals." —Kelly Chen, former mentee, senior audit associate, KPMG

- "Just knowing that I have someone who has experienced situations similar to mine feels like a pocket ace every time I face an obstacle." —Ethan Harris, former mentee, senior project coordinator, Xator Corporation

- "I have learned not to be afraid of failure...when John [her mentor] admitted to some failures, it made it easier for me to talk with him. He would often say,

'These are the things that I have done in my life. This is what worked, and this was what succeeded.' That really helped me get out of my comfort zone and progress with my life." —Morgan Peppers, former mentee, graduate assistant, UWF College of Business

- "The Executive Mentor Program was the most transformative thing for me. I learned how to make relationships, and build them, and encapsulate the humanity that we have as people and our experiences and build on that with others. You just can't get that out of a textbook." —Sarah Lee, former mentee, revenue operations coordinator, IMS Consulting & Expert Services

As mentioned before, don't make participation in your mentoring program compulsory for employees. They might not be ready. Mandating involvement can feel like punishment or imply they aren't doing everything expected of them. It might also feel like you are simply stacking one more thing to do onto their already full plate.

Pressuring employees to be mentees will not create buy-in or enthusiasm for the program. People who participate without passion are unlikely to engage effectively with their mentors and will simply "go through the motions." None of this will further your cause of creating a thriving program that benefits your organization and enjoys long-term support of senior leaders and other stakeholders!

Thoughtfully Match for a Successful Connection

A successful mentoring relationship depends on thoughtful matchmaking. "Assignment mentoring" in a corporate or collegiate environment is risky unless the assigner carefully screens for fit. It's especially important that mentee needs match mentor resources and that there are common interests that result in a personal connection between the two. It's a delicate balance.

You can tell a suitable pairing has been made when a mentor and mentee like and respect one another, get along well together, and seem to have plenty to discuss—and when the mentee seems positively challenged.

✓ Success Secret: The Ideal Experience Gap Is 10-20 Years

This far out, the mentor is experienced, but can still remember what it felt like to be in their mentee's shoes. In addition, sometimes it's difficult for a mentee to accept advice from someone their same age, regardless of the other's experience.

James Hosman, one of our founding executive mentors and market president of Centennial Bank, shares, "I think it is critically important to match a mentor with a mentee who can relate to each other without the mentee feeling like they were matched with someone who does not have adequate experience. Although I had plenty of experience, I was matched with a mentee who was the same age as myself. Regardless of my level of experience, I think it was hard for the mentee to look at me as anything but an equal rather than a mentor. For that particular student, a mentor with a larger age gap may have been more appropriate."

A well-thought-out matching process helps participants begin their journey with a distinct advantage: a high likelihood of establishing a strong rapport. Be aware that matching can be one of the trickiest aspects of a mentoring program. We're all human. People bring with them various backgrounds, values, communication styles, and needs. Everyone is different. An excellent match for one person may be a bad match for another.

✗ Potential Pitfall: Not Investing the Time to Get It Right, Resulting in Mismatched Pairs

Matching mentors and mentees can be the trickiest part of getting your mentoring program right. Using the wrong matching model could produce dissatisfied participants and, ultimately, low participation. Mentoring programs that have fallen apart over this step often misjudged the time it takes to match mentors and mentees effectively. Don't underestimate the time needed to make meaningful matches.

So what can the program champion do up front to make it more likely that this rapport will happen? Over the next pages, we'll cover four steps that will go a long way toward meeting this goal. They are:

1. Decide on your method of matching.

2. Intelligently match based on profiles.

3. Connect the mentor and mentee.

4. Trust but verify.

Decide on Your Method of Matching: Self-Match, Admin-Match, or My Version

One of the first questions to ask yourself is how to match people to achieve an authentic connection and a strong, mutually beneficial relationship. For real mentorship to happen, there needs to be a baseline chemistry between a mentor and a mentee.

Here are a few common approaches:

Informal Self-Match. I don't recommend this approach. Some mentoring programs let the mentees self-match with mentors of their choosing with no guidance from the organization. These re-lationships develop out of common interests and agreeable personalities. That's nice and requires little work from your or-ganization. However, there can be significant drawbacks:

- Younger people may feel intimidated by the person who is actually the best mentor fit, so they don't ask.
- Popular senior leaders may be inundated with requests for mentoring and accept too many.
- Shy, introverted, or less visible senior leaders may be over-looked by mentees even though they would be a good fit.

If your company is already using the self-match method, consider incorporating Sherry's Selection Process (below) into your pro-gram management.

Formal Admin-Match. I don't recommend the basic form of this method, either. In an organizational setting, it is often desirable to develop a formal mentoring program to ensure that some mentoring is occurring. Unfortunately, these formal mentor-ships often include a forced pairing that is made with very little (or no) regard for compatibility. Organizations may assign someone in management to mentor a lower-level employee as part of their job.

This system simply doesn't work well. According to one study, "formally assigned mentorships are known to result in less iden-tification, less relational comfort, less motivation for mentoring, and ultimately, less communication and interaction." (Johnson) Also, randomly assigning students to a mentor is usually associ-ated with the lowest degree of success. (Cesa and Fraser)

Sherry's Selection Process. The matching process we use at UWF has been successful because we give serious thought to which mentor is the best fit for which mentee, and vice versa.

Our system translates easily to other types of organizations. At the heart of our system is a willingness to give the person responsible for the organization's mentoring program:

- Flexibility and scope in deciding who should be matched on what criteria
- Time to get to know—at least a bit about—every mentor and every mentee, to understand their needs and to make the best matches

Think about it: At the core of mentoring is relationship-building. You cannot foster strong relationships if you don't know the parties in question.

It is important to give mentees a say in the type of person they'd like to have as a mentor (such as someone in a specific field or job function, with a particular background or skillset) through their application and during an interview.

Also, give mentors a say in the matching process by first having them outline their interests in their application form and during their interview. Make the process easy for the mentor by culling through all the possible mentees to find the top two or three candidates who are likely to be the best fit for them. Then, allow the mentor to choose a mentee from the narrowed field—creating buy-in for the mentor and commitment to their mentee.

This part of the process, and the rest of the steps laid out in this chapter, reflect our approach at UWF.

Intentionally Match Based on Profiles

Best practices for matching start with having valuable information about the participants (mentors and mentees). As you recruit people for the program, gather essential data about each person. Critical profile elements include educational background, career path, development goals, outside interests, experiences, challenges, and preferences.

Navy Federal
CASE STUDY

The Pairing Process at Navy Federal Credit Union

One of the most critical components of a successful mentoring program is the pairing process. This process is art and science. Consider it carefully.

The Navy Federal mentorship pairings serve to strengthen their mentees' leadership competency development. Mentors and mentees alike identify their leadership competencies on a spectrum that ranges from "a towering strength" to "needs development." Mentees are paired with mentors who possess skill sets that will help the mentee mature and grow in their leadership competency development.

"We have a survey that we send to both mentors and mentees that asks explicit questions to help us try and make the best matches possible," says Thomas Greek of Navy Federal.

A few examples of the leadership competencies included on the survey are: Develops Talent, Strategic Mindset, Drives Vision and Purpose, and Being Resilient.

"This information allows us to understand everyone's expectations and level the playing field," says Greek. "Many participants are grateful that this level of care is given to the selection process and strongly agree that it is what makes the relationship successful."

Two key ways to gather this information are 1) an application form, and 2) an interview. Anyone who wants to participate in the program, whether they are a potential mentor or mentee, fills out an application form. You want to know more unique information than can be found on a résumé or LinkedIn profile.

On the application form, ask for all the pertinent information that will help you find the best match for the participant. While the most substantial correlating factor for engagement is typically shared gender, a few open-ended questions in the application form can provide personal information valuable to the matching process. The answers can uncover common ground, such as a shared love of tennis, or travel, or gourmet cooking, or scuba diving. Mentees and mentors both experience high satisfaction with their matches when they share a "self-description" such as this with each other.

Then, schedule time to talk one-on-one with each person to get to know them, delve deeper into the answers they gave on their application, and ask people to detail what they would like to get out of the program.

Next, match people by common interests and what they want to achieve. For example, you may want to match diverse (in any context) leaders with younger similarly diverse employees, or experienced financial managers with newer financial supervisors. Or you might find two people who love to play tennis. Or you might connect alumni of the same college—this often creates a powerful bond.

✓ Success Secret: Make Connections Based on Profiles and Clear Expectations

Many people say their mentoring experience changed their careers and lives. For mentoring to work well, the mentor and mentee need to have a stable relationship. So, you're probably wondering, what did these successful matches have in common? What was that secret sauce? After observing hundreds of mentor-mentee pairs, here's what I've come to understand distinguished the most successful duos from the rest:

- Matches were made based on backgrounds, interests, and areas of expertise.

- Both parties clearly understood the expectations of the program.

I have learned from experience, living here in Pensacola, you don't want to make the mistake of pairing rival college alumni and supporters! Florida State University Seminoles and University of Miami Hurricanes just aren't going to immediately bond. Neither are 'Bama and Auburn alumni.

The goal is to find common interests that can help to jump-start conversations and bonding. The more you know about your mentees and mentors, the better chance of a great fit and an enjoyable, productive mentoring outcome.

To kindle rapport at UWF, we review all the information we have by hand, and pair people who are like-minded and have similar interests and areas of expertise. Even though there are automated methods to do this type of matching, we feel it is essential to hand-select the pairs to produce the best matchups.

This isn't personality matching—it's common-ground matching—and it works well because it helps jump-start the relationship.

UWF
CASE STUDY

Great Matchmaking Matters!

One female mentee at UWF wanted career development advice specific to accounting and was looking for a mentor who was a working mom with a successful career. We paired her with a senior female executive who started her career in an accounting firm and moved into a CFO role while raising two children.

One fun aspect of this match was that they both graduated from the same high school and college—

something neither would have known without our asking the questions and pairing them. They spent time talking about the different opportunities in the accounting industry, the career paths available, and how to blend work life with family life, which empowered the mentee to take ownership of her career journey.

Connect the Mentor and Mentee

At UWF, I generally whittle down the list of potential mentees to the best two or three candidates. Then I share the possible mentees' applications with the mentor to review before they select one. Not only does this save a lot of time for the mentor, it creates buy-in. They want to help this person.

Once the mentor has chosen a mentee, it's time for that important first meeting. I've learned it's more effective to have the mentee take ownership of the process. Ownership often makes for a valuable learning experience for the mentee and can build confidence.

First, tell the mentee that you are happy to share with them that "X" [mentor name and title] has chosen them. It makes anyone feel good and special to know that someone has specifically chosen them—and helps kick off their relationship in a positive way. Then, ask the mentee to call the mentor in the next few days to introduce himself or herself and schedule the first meeting. Having this responsibility to drive the relationship is a good learning experience for the mentee. It also takes some of the pressure off of the mentor.

I often get the question from younger adults, Why a phone call? Isn't that old-fashioned? My response is that a phone call is more polite, professional, and personal. While many of us prefer other modes of communication, whether it is emails, texting, or messaging, the mentee needs to remember that their mentor may be from a generation that is more comfortable with phone calls.

I have been surprised by how many younger mentees are hesitant to make that call. In addition to being more comfortable with texts and messaging, they are often nervous about reaching out to the highly successful "out of their league" mentor. I tell these mentees, this is the easiest call you'll ever make! This mentor picked you, wants to help you, and is expecting and waiting for you to call. I also encourage the mentee to write a simple script for the call, if that will help.

Trust but Verify

You must trust that the mentees and mentors in your program are doing what they agreed to do in the program. However, verify it. Check in on the mentors and mentees, separately, to confirm that the mentee has called the mentor and that they have had their first meeting. You don't want the mentor waiting and waiting, with no call made. And you also don't want to have a mentee calling and calling with no response from the mentor, or no meeting scheduled.

If the matching process is well designed, mismatches should occur relatively infrequently—10 percent at most for the total number of pairs. Sometimes a mismatch is a personality clash that you couldn't predict. Other times the mismatch is due to someone's not fulfilling their commitment to the program (missing scheduled meeting times, etc.).

Yet for the most part, if you invest the time to carefully pair up mentees and mentors, based on backgrounds, expertise, areas of interest, and common ground, you can feel good about the odds of a successful match.

A Few Mentorship Success Stories

Feedback from mentors and mentees:

"When DaCotah [her mentee] and I were first matched, it was obvious from the very beginning that it was a perfect match—that we were meant to be paired together."

> —Amy Miller, mentor, deputy city administrator for administration & enterprises, City of Pensacola, FL

"I think that the most valuable thing that I have gained through this program is the opportunity to have a lifelong friend that I can always reach out to and check up on and help her with any kind of questions that she may have professionally or personally in her life."

> —Pam Hatt, mentor, vice president of marketing, Pen Air Federal Credit Union

"Morgan [her mentee] reminded me why the millennials may be the coolest generation ever! They are the exciting, energizing, idea-generating, anything-is-possible group of people that we boomers raised them to be."

> —Becca Boles, mentor, corporate communications director, Gulf Power Company

I'd like to end with the words of Simon Sinek, author of *Start with Why: How Great Leaders Inspire Everyone to Take Action*: "Building a mentor relationship is like building a friendship—it develops over time like a good friendship and both people must equally invest in the relationship. Because believe it or not, both are learning from it." (Sinek)

Abbajay, Mary. "Mentoring Matters: Three Essential Elements of Success." 2019.

Cesa, Ian L and Scott C Fraser. "A Method for Encouraging the Development of Good Mentor-Protégé Relationships." *Teaching of Psychology*, vol. 16, 1989.

Drucker, Peter F. *Management: Tasks, Responsibilities, Practices.* Routledge, 2012.

Johnson, W. Brad. "The Intentional Mentor: Strategies and Guidelines for the Practice of Mentoring." *Professional Psychology: Research and Practice*, vol. 33, 2002, p. 89.

Koifman, Natasha. "Don't have a mentor? Then mentor yourself." 2016.

Murphy, Wendy. "Propelling Women's Careers: A Developmental Network Approach." *Women in Leadership Conference*, University of West Florida, 2017.

Murphy, Wendy and Kathy Kram. *Strategic Relationships at Work.* McGraw-Hill Education, 2014.

Sinek, Simon. *Start with Why: How Great Leaders Inspire Everyone to Take Action.* Portfolio, 2009.

Tjan, Anthony K. "What the Best Mentors Do." 2017.

Wooden, John and Don Yaeger. *A Game Plan for Life.* Bloomsbury, 2011.

CHAPTER 13

Step 6: Nurture Your People and Your Program

Now that your mentors and mentees are on board and matched, the real action begins. Finding and making the right match is a terrific feeling, but you can't expect the program to function on autopilot after launch. Your program must be set up to help nurture the connections being made. You must find ways to invite regular feedback from each participant along the way and look for opportunities to improve processes.

Left to themselves, many mentorships will flourish. But some may not. Why? Because mentoring is not usually part of one's everyday routine. Without direction, the mentoring relationship is vulnerable to losing focus and momentum.

I like what George Bernard Shaw said about communication: "The single biggest problem in communication is the illusion that it has taken place."(Creech) Mentoring is the same. Don't assume all is well just because you set the wheels in motion. Providing guidance throughout the mentorship is vital to a successful mentoring program.

Offer Training and Reinforcement Throughout the Program for Both Mentors and Mentees

Mentoring isn't always intuitive. Getting started on the right foot can take a little getting used to, especially for someone new to mentoring. At the very least, you should explain the foundations of your program up front and thoroughly. You don't want your mentors or mentees to feel lost or unprepared. It will lead to a poor experience and can cause people to drop out of the program. But if you reinforce the training throughout the program, it's even more beneficial.

Training reinforcement can include creating opportunities for mentors and mentees to get together, such as learning from a keynote speaker at a meeting and exchanging ideas about what they've just heard. Mentors can help mentees practice what they are learning from a mentor on a work project, or practice networking skills at a meet-and-greet event. And, don't forget the value of having the mentor program provide bite-size "mentoring lessons" in regular communications with participants, such as in an e-newsletter.

Why invest time in training? Research by one of the international pioneers of coaching and mentoring, Professor David Clutterbuck, has shown that only one in three mentoring relationships are successful when mentors or mentees get no instruction. That figure increases to two in three relationships succeeding when the mentors have professional training in how to be a good mentor. The most impactful training scenario, however, is when both participants receive training, in which case, there is a 90 percent success rate. (Clutterbuck)

This book offers many key points that should be included in training for both mentors and mentees: Bert's icebreaker questions and the Eight Great Social Tells (Chapter 3); self-assessment learning, adult learner preferences, and discussion tips for mentees (Chapter 11); and the tips in the rest of this chapter.

Conduct Orientation Sessions

Invite all new participants to orientation sessions. Make attendance easy for them. During the meetings, provide training to new mentors and new mentees about:

- Why you created the program
- The program's goals
- Benefits to mentees, mentors, the organization
- Eligibility requirements for mentees and mentors
- Responsibilities of participants
- Mentoring best practices and tips
- Any other significant aspects of the program

Here are a few tips from my own experience in conducting these training sessions:

1. Do not have new mentors and new mentees in the same orientation sessions. Separating them gives the mentors and the mentees the freedom to be more frank and open in their discussions.

2. Cover the same crucial training points in both sessions. The goal is full transparency. Make sure what you're telling the mentors about the program is the same as what you're telling the mentees. It keeps everyone on the same page.

3. Invite experienced mentors to join the new mentor orientation sessions to share stories and advice. Likewise, invite experienced mentees to join the new mentee sessions. Enable the newbies to learn and hear from people who have "been there,

done that." The stories you hear regarding their prior experiences are often enlightening and impactful.

Caution all parties that the mentor's task is to guide the mentee, not secure the mentee an internship, job, or promotion. (FYI: Sometimes people get confused about the difference between a mentorship and an internship. In a college setting, internships are career-based learning experiences that involve a "real-world" work environment and standard workplace expectations. Mentorships are business relationships where an expert coaches and guides a newcomer to the field. Typically, mentorships are unpaid—but the one-on-one time is incredibly valuable.)

Success Factors to Weave into Your Training

Emphasize these essential points in your onboarding sessions and training materials for both mentors and mentees. Understanding these success factors will help ensure that program participants go on to develop healthy relationships with one another:

- **Trust.** Mentors and mentees must believe in the reliability and truthfulness of one another. When trust is present, mentors will willingly contribute what is needed by sharing honest thoughts on how the mentee is performing. A mentee has to trust that conversations with mentors don't have an echo; in other words, that honest conversation doesn't get back to their boss or to HR. There is great value to the organization in getting feedback from mentees. It can reveal strengths and weaknesses inside the company, but that won't happen without trust.
- **An Alliance Mentality.** The working relationship is a partnership between a mentor and mentee; this includes: 1) the bond, a professional relationship built on trust, 2) agreement on the goal they'll be jointly pursuing, and 3) an understanding of the activities necessary to achieve

those goals. The alliance builds on initial trust, a commitment to collaboration, and mutual goal selection.

- **Empathy.** This implies not just sensing another's feelings and emotions but understanding and seeing things from their perspective. While both parties need empathy, it's probably most important for mentors. They will need to call on it to read and attend to their mentees' needs and help alleviate any anxiety they may be feeling. Mentors can show empathy by focusing on their mentees' many attributes, assets, and strengths, rather than what they don't know or can't do.

- **Positive Expectations.** When we expect to be successful, we do the things that make us successful. There is great power in positive expectations. Both the mentor and the mentee need to go into their partnership assuming their relationship will be a productive, rewarding one. When they do, the rest takes care of itself.

- **Sensitivity to Cultural Differences and a Willingness to Help with Adaptations.** Mentees of diverse ethnic and racial groups may have values and perspectives that differ from the majority of the organization. Mentors can help them culturally adapt to expectations such as how to tackle problems and solutions, participate in meetings, and build professional relationships.

- **Mentor Humility.** The best mentors are open to learning from the mentoring program AND from their mentees and are willing to ask for advice when they need it. Both parties go into the relationship with the expectation that the mentor is going to "teach" the mentee, but mentors need to remember that they don't know it all. Stay open to learning how to better mentor AND be willing to learn from the mentee—it's a two-way street.

The need for instruction and guidance doesn't end after the orientation session. You'll want to provide tips and best practices throughout the year to help mentors and mentees remain on track and get the most out of the program. I do this by sending short emails to participants with quick tips and friendly reminders.

Help Mentors and Mentees Understand the Change Process

Your purpose for wanting to create a mentoring program is to help the mentees grow and change to reach their full potential. Embracing change isn't always easy. Helping others to embrace change is occasionally frustrating.

There are various causes for resistance to change. (Kotter and Schlesinger) The pitfalls listed below often manifest themselves in the workplace, but if one has a mentor, the mentor can help the mentee understand why they feel this resistance to change. This gives the mentee an extra tool to overcome their resistance. Part of the process assists the mentor in understanding what the mentee could be going through, but the other part is that the mentor can help the mentee become more self-aware by educating them on the "why."

A few reasons why people resist change:

- **Parochial Self-Interest.** When the president of a manufacturing company announces a new, flatter organizational structure, a frustrated mentee thinks she will lose her opportunity to move into a supervisory position this year.
- **Misunderstanding and Lack of Trust.** For example, when a vice president begins approving new staff to one department and stalls the replacement of open positions in the mentee's department, with no explanation as to why, the mentee is frustrated. His trust in the company wanes.
- **Different Individual Assessments/Perceptions of Change and a Lower Tolerance for Change.** Some people fear they will not be able to develop the new skills and behavior

required of them. This was especially prevalent with senior leaders when the COVID-19 pandemic of 2020 forced nearly everyone to—abruptly—work remotely. Some did not agree with this change and were frustrated by the new technical skills required.

In all of these instances, mentors need a good understanding of the trajectory of change so that they can a) not get so frustrated themselves when the mentee doesn't seem to "get it," and b) reassure the mentee that change is uncomfortable and takes time.

To achieve meaningful change, mentors need a simple way to understand and influence change in their mentees, identify causes of resistance, and help individuals successfully transition. One change management philosophy is the ADKAR model. (Hiatt) It is an acronym that represents the five tangible and concrete outcomes that people need to achieve for lasting change:

- Awareness—of the need for change
- Desire—to support the change
- Knowledge—of how to change
- Ability—to demonstrate skills and behaviors
- Reinforcement—to make the change stick

As an illustration of change needed for mentors and mentees (that had the potential to be strongly resisted) at UWF was the—literally overnight—change from an in-person mentoring program to a virtual one. This wasn't simply managing resistance to change from one person, but managing it for potentially more than 120 people at once. But, the same principles apply.

Awareness. While the best way to overcome resistance to change is to educate people about it beforehand, obviously this wasn't an option. However, we did rapidly provide education and communication (via emails and phone calls) with all participants so they would see the need for and logic of the change.

Desire. We worked to gain participation and involvement in designing and implementing the change to virtual, by actively seeking input from all participants (via emails, phone calls, and virtual meetings), and by listening to them and using their advice.

Knowledge. We quickly developed and made available to mentors and mentees an entire "tool kit" of materials to provide training and tips on virtual mentoring, tutorials on how to use new technologies, and how to provide emotional support. These efforts on the part of our program staff were time-consuming but worthwhile.

Ability. Simply providing training materials and tutorials isn't enough. We also provided our mentors and mentees with an opportunity to learn, and use hands-on, various new online meeting technology tools as a group. We hosted virtual events using a variety of software programs (Zoom, Google Meet, Remo, Wonder) to increase our mentors' and mentees' comfort and abilities.

Reinforcement. In all of our virtual meetings, we included select mentors and mentees who provided input into the design and implementation of the virtual meetings, and who often played a visible role. This helped gain individual and group support. We reinforced the value of these changes by keeping the need for the change top of mind, while also showing successful results as an upshot of the change along the way.

Mentors who follow this model step-by-step can help facilitate the mentee's change journey.

✓ Success Secret: Keep It Challenging

In any mentorship, there should be a certain level of challenge. Otherwise, it risks being non-impactful.

Empower the Mentee to Drive the Relationship

At UWF, the mentee is responsible for taking charge of the relationship with the mentor. That means reaching out to the mentor to set the time and date of the meetings at their mutual convenience. We make sure they understand that they co-own the relationship and that they are equally—if not more—responsible for making sure it works.

During the mentee's orientation sessions with the program staff, and in the training materials we give them, we talk about setting an agenda for meetings with their mentor and having questions prepared in advance to ask during the meeting. We even provide pages and pages of potential questions they could ask their mentor to help get conversations started.

The mentor-mentee meetings are all as different as the individuals involved. Some mentors lead the meetings, while others leave it to the mentees to lead the meetings. And that's okay. Some of the mentees find it a scary prospect to be one-on-one with the CEO of a company. During the orientation, we empower the mentees to feel confident, to appreciate that these meetings are about them and their professional development. Their growth and success are why the mentor is there. We teach them that it is acceptable, and even necessary, to be prepared to take the lead in driving the conversations around their needs.

Here's a bright idea that I learned from another company: Give each mentee a Starbucks gift card so they can "buy" if they set up a coffee meeting with their mentor. Having the gift card also encourages pairs to get off campus, or out of the office, where they can have casual and more private conversations.

Encourage Mentees (with Their Mentors) to Establish Personal Goals and Action Plans

A best practice is to encourage the mentees to ask themselves, *What do I want and need help with?* before they sit down with their mentor. Knowing this helps a mentorship get off to a good start and adds a little accountability to accomplish something. With that said, let me share with you my most significant "ah-ha!" moment at UWF. Often, college students, and likely some of your employees, don't know what they don't know!

They Don't Know What They Don't Know

After a couple of decades in the working world, I assumed everyone knew these facts, but they don't necessarily. Many didn't know that they didn't know that…

- Business is built on relationships. It doesn't matter if you will be a CPA and work with numbers all day; if you want to be successful in business, you have to master the soft skill of forming bonds with people.
- Dressing for success is a real thing. I was always told to "dress for the job you want, not the one you have" and to watch the people who are in the positions you'd like to have one day, how they dress and how they present themselves.
- In the workplace, there are no participation points. Just because you gave it your best effort doesn't mean you deserve the job or a raise.
- Doing well in school, and having a 4.0, will not automatically get you the job you want after graduation. You need to reach out to businesses, get real hands-on experience, and do informational interviews.
- Your first job won't be your last job. I talk with students who agonize about making the wrong choice, thinking that if they choose wrong on the first job, they will have a

horrible career path forever. Times have changed. Lifelong employment is a thing of the past. So don't stress about picking the perfect job right away.

- "Networking" is not a dirty word. Some students think "networking" is all about "schmoozing" and being pushy. They don't realize it's about relationship-building and connecting with people to help each other. It's a reciprocal—not one-way—relationship.

Build Trust Through Regular Meetings

It is natural that mentees may want to call their mentors when something comes up, or they get stuck. We support those calls. In these situations, mentors generally provide off-the-cuff advice that may be adequate. However, regular meetings empower duos to come prepared and make incremental progress toward bigger goals—while nurturing the relationship and building a level of trust that results in real success. Checking in periodically to make sure these regular meetings are happening is one way the program champion helps nurture the mentoring relationship.

The key is not to impose rigid or unrealistic expectations. Everyone is busy, particularly accomplished executives. We suggest participants set a loose guideline—such as once a month for a year—not "in my office every other Tuesday at 9:00 a.m." Structured flexibility is more realistic on both sides, and minor rescheduling when things come up, research papers are due, or fires break out won't derail momentum.

Participants should measure progress on the previously discussed goals and action plans at every meeting. Have pairs set aside five or ten minutes at the beginning of their meetings to talk about what happened since they last met. What progress has been made toward the goal that was defined? If they had to quantify it, what would they say? Maybe they're 30 percent there? Eighty percent?

Having this type of conversation is helpful for both mentors and mentees. It provides momentum and helps in establishing benchmarks. For example, they can discuss what would take the mentee from 25 percent to 40 percent by the time of the next conversation.

"I think part of the reason why my mentor/mentee relationships have been successful is that we lay out goals that the mentee and I both agree on in the beginning. We review those goals every time we meet and ensure that we are making progress on accomplishing them. It's difficult to know if you are meeting expectations if you've not properly set them in the beginning."

—James Hosman, UWF alumnus; executive mentor; market president, Centennial Bank

Provide Relevant Support Resources and Assess Progress

The best mentoring programs provide appropriate support resources at strategic points in the mentorship to help guide and nurture the relationship and the learning. As time progresses, check in with all participants to gauge their progress as well as to track whether mentees are reaching out to their mentors so that, if necessary, you can gently intervene.

At UWF, we don't formally track the details of each pair's efforts and initiatives. Still, we find that simply the act of reporting progress back to us helps mentors and mentees stay productive and on course. Or, if they have lost a little focus, it prompts them to reconnect and get back on track.

Go back to the materials and support resources created for your mentoring program and determine the optimal timeframe to share specific resources with participants. For example, a Best Practices Guide is most helpful at the beginning of the process — perfect for orientation and onboarding. A Tips Guide on asking open-ended questions to spark productive conversations—getting the mentee to open up—might be more valuable after the pairs have met a few times.

We send monthly email newsletters to participants that highlight upcoming events and important dates, and also provide articles and links to resources that can spark conversations for their one-on-one meetings and encourage personal growth. We use this communication channel to offer support, spur engagement, and assess progress. You can use this communication channel to encourage participants to work on their "Learn List" (that Bert discussed previously) for the next 30-day and 12-month time increments.

Set Clear Checkpoints

Clear checkpoints help the participants appreciate there is a beginning, middle, and end to the program. Although this may sound basic, we have found this is a significant factor in satisfaction for many participants in our mentoring program. Ambiguity can be uncomfortable for some.

- **Beginning.** Make this obvious and memorable. This includes both the orientation sessions as well as a welcome event. Signal a definite start to give the momentum needed to get the relationship off the ground.
- **Middle.** This is based on the program length you communicated to your mentors and mentees when they enrolled in the program. At UWF, the program typically runs eight to twelve months, coinciding with the academic school year, so the middle is around month five or six. During this time, it is imperative to look for red flags that indicate a relationship might not be working. Often a phone call or meeting is sufficient to notice failing connections and either help them get back on track or help them to jointly decide the mentorship isn't going to be mutually beneficial.

- **End.** Have a formal process that brings closure to the mentoring experience. Within this process, provide participants the opportunity to reflect upon their successes, what they learned, next steps, and benefits of the program. Include both outcome evaluation surveys as well as a year-end or conclusion event, which signals a bright end to this chapter and provides an opportunity for well-deserved recognition and celebration.

In the best mentoring relationships, as Bert wrote earlier, it's never really over. The formal program pairing may conclude, but, hopefully, the informal professional relationship pairs have established will last forever.

✗ Potential Pitfall: Too Much or Not Enough Structure

Create structure, but not too much. It's important to remember that everyone is different. Different people require different situations to feel at ease. Some participants will appreciate access to tools and resources when they are beginning their mentoring relationship, and others will feel overly pressured if they are required to use them.

I'm a big believer in the "tight-loose-tight" model to offer both structure and flexibility. This approach empowers people while ensuring the desired outcomes. To briefly explain:

- The first "tight" component has to do with everyone clearly understanding the goals, objectives, expectations, and the role they play. This structure provides mentors and mentees a workflow to follow.

- Being "loose" in the middle empowers mentors and mentees to get on with it, their way, now that they know the big picture. Flexibility is essential to support different mentoring needs across learning goals, preferences, and learning styles.

- The final "tight" component drives success by ensuring accountability. Inspect what you expect. As President Ronald Reagan said, "Trust but verify." Your program leader must check in with mentors and mentees frequently.

"It's the 'tight-loose-tight' structure," says serial entrepreneur and executive mentor Robert Bennett when explaining why the Executive Mentor Program at UWF works. "Define expectations and allow people to figure out how to achieve the objectives in their style, approach, priorities...etc. However, the student should feel free to seek reinforcement from the manager, and the manager should periodically check in with the mentor and the mentee."

For a mentoring program to work, it needs to be flexible enough to evolve with the relationship, and it also requires some boundaries and expectations to maintain momentum.

Embrace Opportunities for Reverse Mentoring

Here I use "reverse mentoring" NOT to mean that younger people are serving as mentors to older ones in an official capacity (although, as discussed earlier, this is a very valid practice). Instead, I am talking about older mentors making a point to learn from mentees even as they mentor them.

Encourage your mentors to stay open to learning, too; this provides value to them and keeps them more engaged. As Buzz Ritchie, one of our founding executive mentors, says, "If an individual serves as a mentor, he probably gets as much or more out of it than the student does. It isn't really so much me sitting here telling him about what he should or shouldn't do; we exchange ideas all the time."

For some mentors, participating in UWF's Executive Mentor Program is a way to learn from someone in the generation currently entering the workforce.

"I think we can all learn something from the younger generation, their outlook on career, life, and priorities," says executive mentor Ron Jackson, CPA, shareholder and past president of Saltmarsh, Cleaveland & Gund. "It always helps management learn how to manage the younger segment of the workforce. I have learned that unlike the time when I came into the workforce, not all graduates will sacrifice time and social life to be successful in their profession. I guess that's due to the prosperity experienced by the younger generation; the desire to succeed and the definition of success have shifted a lot."

Other executive mentors at UWF have said they want to connect with today's tech-savvy generation to better understand how they are using new and emerging tools and technology. For example, what apps are they using for productivity? The savviest mentors know that you really can teach an old dog new tricks. Mentors, if you can devote some of your mentoring session time to being that "old dog," so much the better.

Mutual Mentorship Powers Digital Transformation

An organization seeking to adapt to digital disruption needs mentors at every level. Younger, more digitally savvy employees can help senior managers in this arena, creating new opportunities for cross-generational discovery and development. Digital transformation changes how we think about people, customers, and approaches to training and mentoring programs. Recent research suggests that employees expect digital transformation to better reflect and respect their concerns and values, not just boost business capabilities and opportunities. (Schrage et al.)

Digital transformation requires digital leadership. Leaders must measurably transform themselves to become digitally savvy, and reverse mentorship is a viable way to accomplish this. Not doing so undermines a leader's capabilities and credibility. Opening themselves up, and admitting they need help, isn't always easy.

Chip Conley, a hotelier and former Airbnb executive, was quoted in the *MIT Sloan Management Review* as saying, "Someone can feel like an idiot because they need help to understand Slack. The future of leadership is all about mutual mentorship. The best leaders are great learners." Leaders must learn, he says, "how to be confident and vulnerable, because these are not mutually exclusive." (Schrage et al.)

Marvin Bower, who helped build McKinsey & Company and is considered the father of modern management consulting, defined culture as "the way we do things around here." (Bower) By his definition, digital transformation—the new way we do things around here—is cultural. Leaders must ensure that digital transformation strengthens the organization's cultural values (such as integrity and being customer-centric) and avoids options that can damage the organization (such as choosing cost-cutting over customer experience). (Schrage et al.)

Ensure Your Mentoring Program Is Scalable Yet Manageable

While it is advantageous to have a scalable program, the program mustn't be so extensive that it begins to lose quality and prestige. There is no one sweet spot. It depends on many factors: how many people-hours you have to manage the program, how much experience your program manager has, and how extensive your mentoring program is in terms of scope (including activities you provide, communications you manage, benchmarks you select to measure).

Thomas Greek from Navy Federal Credit Union, speaking from the perspective of a large organization, says: "With larger programs, you run the risk of one mentor having to work with multiple participants, thus diminishing the quality of the relationship.

Since mentors have day-to-day responsibilities, they might not be able to prioritize several relationships at once. You also run the risk of not having enough mentors for the number of mentees who are interested in the program, causing you to consider relaxing your mentor selection criteria to meet the demands. Finally, with larger groups, program managers may not have the ability to continue personal touchpoints, which is a proven way to ensure program success."

I caution you not to make your program so big that you can't provide proper oversight. As I have detailed, there is a lot involved in having a successful program, including regular interaction with mentors and mentees.

Finally, Provide Recognition for Participation

Celebrating success and recognizing milestone achievements is an essential part of any project. Formally recognizing mentor involvement, internally and to the public, can be very motivating and help attract additional mentors to the program. You want to create a program where the mentors are considered an influential, successful group of leaders, and the mentees are considered rising stars full of potential.

To recognize, celebrate, and thank mentors and mentees, you could provide appreciation gifts, photos of the mentor and mentee together, and thank-you cards signed by senior leaders and the program champion. You could tell their stories and feature participants in newsletters, in press releases, on your website, and on social media. Your program could host an appreciation event, a mix-and-mingle, a breakfast, a luncheon, or a dinner. You could recognize a mentor and mentee of the year with awards and present them at the appreciation event. Regardless of what you choose, saying "thank you" is the simplest and most important way to show your appreciation.

Appreciation Quotes for Thank-Yous

- "We ourselves feel that what we are doing is just a drop in the ocean. But the ocean would be less because of that missing drop."

  —Mother Teresa (Teresa)

- "No act of kindness, no matter how small, is ever wasted."
  —Aesop (Aesop)

- "Everybody can be great, because everybody can serve."
  —Martin Luther King Jr. (King)

- "Never doubt that a small group of thoughtful, committed citizens can change the world; indeed, it's the only thing that ever has."

  —Margaret Mead (Keys)

Finally, remember that communication is the "golden thread" that weaves through the entire program implementation and management. We emphasize transparency and two-way communication structures that provide avenues to vent frustrations, applaud what is working, and seamlessly change what doesn't work.

As program champion, keep this truth in mind at all times. Be visible. Be vocal. And never stop looking for ways to advocate for your program and celebrate the mentors and mentees who make it work.

Aesop. *The Fables of Aesop.* Calla Editions, 2014. Edward Detmold.
Bower, Marvin. *The Will to Manage: Corporate Success through Programmed Management.* McGraw-Hill, 1966.

Clutterbuck, David. "Establishing and Maintaining Mentoring Relationships: An Overview of Mentor and Mentee Competencies." *SA Journal of Human Resource Management*, vol. 3, 2005.

Creech, Bill. *The Five Pillars of TQM: How to Make Total Quality Management Work for You.* Plume, 1995.

Hiatt, Jeffrey M. *ADKAR: A Model for Change in Business, Government and Our Community.* Prosci Learning Center Publications, 2006.

Keys, Donald. *Earth at Omega: Passage to Planetization.* THE BRANDEN PRESS, 1982.

King, Jr., Martin Luther. "The Drum Major Instinct Sermon." Stanford University, The Martin Luther King, Jr. Research and Education Institute, 1968.

Kotter, John P and Leonard A Schlesinger. "Choosing Strategies for Change." *Harvard Business Review*, 2008.

Schrage, Michael et al. "Leadership's Digital Transformation: Leading Purposefully in an Era of Context Collapse." *MIT Sloan Management Review*, 2021.

Teresa, Mother. *Where There Is Love, There Is God.* Image, 2012

CHAPTER 14

Step 7: Measure to Improve

It's easy to get your mentoring program up and running, pat yourself on the back, and think you are done. But if you do, you've missed a critical step. If your goal is to provide effective mentoring that changes each mentee's life for the better—and this *should* be your goal—then you must confirm that the mentoring is effective through program evaluation and metrics.

Management guru Peter Drucker says, "If you can't measure it, you can't improve it." *In the case of mentoring programs, you can't know whether or not it is successful unless success is defined and tracked. If you don't monitor results, you'll have no idea if you are succeeding or not.* It's like me trying to improve my golf game. If I never keep score, I might be (much) happier in the short-term, but I'll never know if I'm getting better or not.

Measure what matters to ensure great results, just like you would with any other important piece of your business. This will help you generate both short-term wins and long-term improvement.

A few chapters back, we talked about setting goals for your program. Understanding how the mentoring program you created measures up to your expectations may be the most important step of all. Measure your program based on the actionable metrics you established.

- Evaluate: What's working? What's not?
- Assess: What do you still need to know?

Your mentoring program must show a real impact. If not, it becomes a nice-to-have initiative, and as with most nice-to-have initiatives, it will soon fade away and become a used-to-have.

Without correlating activity to impact, mentoring programs are frequently deemed unnecessary and eliminated long before their real value is realized.

Measure Outcomes at Least Once a Year

Whether capturing results and feedback is accomplished through surveys, performance reviews, or other methods, data is vital to the progression and scalability of your program. Measurement data provides you the opportunity to review, revise, and continuously improve your mentoring program.

To measure UWF's Executive Mentor Program effectiveness, we conduct surveys every year and informally poll and interview participants throughout the year.

I suggest measuring mid-term at least during the first year. This will allow you to a) recognize, collect, and communicate short-term wins, and b) identify trouble spots and opportunities early enough to do something about them.

First, let's talk short-term wins. These are all the small successes that add up to lasting results. Short-term wins are typically in the form of an anecdote or a positive quote from a participant (mentor or mentee) that you can share with the company and other program participants. Recognize, collect, and communicate short-term wins—early and often—to track progress and energize your army of volunteers.

By measuring early, you should be able to gauge what is and isn't working. That way you can make needed changes and adjustments. Let's say, for example, your program requires your paired matches to meet once a week. When you check in with your participants, you find that 1) the weekly meetings aren't happening consistently, and 2) your participants are stressed out because they can't always fit the weekly meetings into their schedules. This isn't setting your participants up for success. Your program champion could change the meeting frequency from once a week to every other week and see how that works.

Evaluate the Right Metrics Tied to Your Objectives

Make sure the right metrics, built around your defined business objectives, are being measured. According to Ben Yoskovitz, the coauthor of Lean Analytics, "Analytics isn't about reporting for the sake of reporting; it's about tracking progress. And not just aimless progress, but progress towards something actionable you're trying to accomplish." (Croll and Yoskovitz)

Cox Communications, for example, measures the progress of their mentoring program on the quality of pairing and experience over the life of the connection. Cox also collects insights on the most impactful activities that mentors and mentees engage in that positively impact learning and growth. And they have a formal net promoter score that their systems capture about Cox's mentoring experience.

If you don't know where you're going, metrics aren't going to be particularly helpful. Even if you can't precisely measure what you want, you can learn about the area with related data. For example, at UWF, we wanted to measure "workforce readiness," which is not something that can be measured precisely. We unpacked the meaning of workforce readiness down to the individual elements, and we measured that related data instead. Our example is below.

UWF
CASE STUDY

How We Measure Workforce Readiness

We measure progress using metrics/elements that define "workforce readiness." Using a written survey once a year, we ask both mentors and mentees the following question. Here is an example of feedback provided by participants in our program:

To what extent do you agree or disagree with the following statements?

Question: The student mentee:	Agree	Neutral	Disagree
has a better understanding of professionalism	91.49%	8.51%	0.00%
has a better understanding of teamwork	72.34%	27.66%	0.00%
has developed his/her leadership skills	76.60%	23.40%	0.00%
has developed more self-confidence	80.43%	19.57%	0.00%
has expanded his/her knowledge of the business community	82.98%	17.02%	0.00%
has gained a better understanding of his/her strengths and weaknesses	78.72%	21.28%	0.00%
has improved his/her verbal communication skills	74.47%	25.53%	0.00%
has improved his/her written communication skills	46.81%	53.19%	0.00%
has increased his/her critical thinking skills	72.34%	27.66%	0.00%
is more prepared to enter the workforce	76.60%	23.40%	0.00%

This quantitative data is easy to understand, and we're quite pleased with the results. However, using only quantitative data sometimes leaves questions begging to be asked. For instance, I was curious to know why roughly half the respondents were only "neutral" regarding whether the mentee had improved their written communication skills. In qualitative follow-up, face-to-face interviews, I asked about the written communication scores. I found that the mentors did not have enough opportunity to read the mentee's writing to form an opinion on whether improvement was made. We learned from this data and the feedback that if we want to measure written communication skills, we need to add writing assignments.

Sounds pretty obvious, right? Until we saw the numbers, though, it was an overlooked opportunity.

> ### UWF
> ## CASE STUDY

A "Stamp of Approval" We Feel Great About!

Within a few years of launching the UWF program, the Association to Advance Collegiate Schools of Business (AACSB) came to Pensacola for a regular audit to reaffirm our college's accreditation. For readers who aren't familiar with higher education credentials, AACSB accreditation represents the highest standard of achievement for business schools worldwide. Less than 5 percent of the more than 16,000 schools worldwide granting business degrees have earned AACSB accreditation.

We were delighted that after reviewing our innovative mentoring program, the AACSB called it a "best practice" and shared our story with accredited schools.

In addition to these kinds of "results" measurements, you also want to gather feedback on the program itself. Is your mentoring timeframe too long, too short, or just right? Are participants taking advantage of the resources you have provided?

Assess a Mix of Both Quantitative and Qualitative Data

As the previous UWF example suggests, measuring a blend of both quantitative and qualitative data will provide a rich and meaningful picture of your program. As I start to discuss quantitative and qualitative data with some of my friends, I can sometimes see their eyes starting to cross—nonetheless, it's not that complicated, and it's absolutely worthwhile. To sum up:

Quantitative data is the numbers. Numbers are easy to track, measure, trend over time, and understand, like sports scores and restaurant star ratings. Quantitative data is objective and precise and answers the "what" questions.

Qualitative data is the words. It's not measured easily; it's what you learn from interviews and discussions. Qualitative data is subjective and imprecise and answers the "how" and "why" questions. While sometimes messy, quotes and excerpts of phrases help paint a picture for you.

For example, Navy Federal Credit Union knows its mentorship program is making an impact due to qualitative data: the rave reviews they are hearing from participants. "We have seen several leaders go through our program, and many of them credit participating in the program as a contributor to their professional and, in some cases, personal success," says Thomas Greek, vice president of learning and development.

When deciding what, and how often, to measure, keep in mind that you want enough information to be able to make sound strategic decisions and to make changes along the way when needed. However, you don't want to weigh your mentoring program down with too much measuring.

✕ Potential Pitfall: Getting Bogged Down in Details

Don't fall into the information-overload trap. Wikipedia says information overload (also known as infobesity, information anxiety, and information explosion) is the difficulty in understanding an issue and effectively making decisions when one has too much information about that issue.

I don't know about you, but my working memory can hold only so much information before it gets overloaded, and I can't see the forest for the trees. One solution to avoid information overload is to avoid vanity metrics as described below.

Another easy trap to fall into is the use of vanity metrics as opposed to actionable metrics. We've discussed actionable metrics already, which are data that tie to specific things you can improve and your organization's goals. Vanity metrics are the opposite. They are things you can measure that make you feel good about what you're doing, but that don't really matter. Vanity metrics can make you look good to others; however, they aren't actionable or related to things you can control in a meaningful way.

For example, at UWF, we could measure the page-views of our Executive Mentor Program website. On the surface, our data could look great. We could have a million people viewing our website pages. I could tell our dean, "Look! We have a million people viewing our pages. We're doing great!" But is that really true? Just by this metric, we wouldn't know. There is no context. There is nothing about that metric that ties with our business goal, and there is nothing actionable we could do with this data to improve our mentoring program in a meaningful way.

Instead, we look at data that focuses on the quality of our program and developing the workforce readiness of students.

While it can be challenging to correlate directly, in addition to key employee retention and other people measures, organizations also tie in overall business success (e.g., revenue growth). Cox Communications and Navy Federal Credit Union both agree that business growth occurred in conjunction with their successful mentoring programs.

If you already have a mentoring program up and running, take a look at the metrics you are using. If a dimension isn't actionable, and you can't do anything to make it better, ask yourself why you are tracking it. What should you track instead?

The moral of this chapter: No matter how much we may love the idea of creating a mentoring program, we simply have to be able to back it up with results. Mentoring is a substantial investment when you consider program groundwork and the valuable time of participants. Telling the impact story is essential to secure on-going funding and long-term support.

The impact story is told through evidence. We show that it's working, that positive results are flowing in, and that human lives are being changed for the better. I am reminded of one of my favorite quotes, often attributed to W. Edwards Deming, "In God we trust. All others must use data." (Walton)

Croll, Alistair and Benjamin Yoskovitz. *Lean Analytics: Use Data to Build a Better Startup Faster*. O'Reilly Media, 2013.
Walton, Mary. *The Deming Management Method*. Perigee Books, 1988.

CHAPTER 15

Epilogue to Part 2 (Sherry's Advice)

Embrace Positive Dissatisfaction

There is an art to mentoring, and I believe the perfect mentoring program is yet to be created. I embrace positive dissatisfaction—meaning that while I'm proud of what we've achieved with UWF's Executive Mentor Program, I want to make it even better. I encourage you also to embrace positive dissatisfaction to enhance acceleration and continuously increase the impact of your mentoring program.

Someone said that *dissatisfaction* is the one-word definition for *motivation*. In the book *Developing the Leader Within You*, John Maxwell wrote that dissatisfied people are highly motivated people because they see the need for change. (Maxwell) The key is harnessing the energy derived from positive dissatisfaction toward effective change.

You've probably heard the phrase from the shampoo commercial "lather, rinse, repeat." Continue to cycle through these seven steps, always giving critical thought to ways to improve your program along the way.

Step 1: Define Your "Why." Decide what it is you want. As Aristotle said, "Are we not more likely to hit the mark if we have a target?" (Aristotle) Know *why* you want it—when you know *what* you want, and you know exactly *why* you want it, you can figure out *how* to get it.

Step 2: Find Your Program Champion. The choice of who will lead your program has a profound impact on the program's strategy, execution, and, ultimately, its performance and success. Clarify the essential qualities needed to succeed and keep an open mind about where the best candidate will come from.

Step 3: Set Goals and Metrics. Creating a mentoring program is an investment in your employees or students. You're allowing them to better understand what they want for their career and life and giving them the chance to develop professionally.

Step 4: Build Your Program. Take action. Have a sense of urgency. The enemy of greatness is perfection. As Dr. Ed Ranelli is fond of saying, "Hustle is a strategy."

Step 5: Recruit and Connect. Mentorships are about creating personal connections and professional relationships. These connections can be invaluable when top performers are considering their next career step. I know that it may sound straightforward and common sense, but what's common sense is not always common practice.

Step 6: Nurture Your People and Your Program. Sustain the acceleration. Continue to initiate change until your vision is a reality.

Step 7: Measure to Improve. Get feedback. Don't underestimate the little things. In the end, little things performed with consistency can lead to significant results over time. Tweak, as needed.

Following these seven steps ensured everything went smoothly for us at UWF as we developed and implemented our Executive Mentor Program. It creates relationships that will last a lifetime and perpetuates the continuing cycle of giving back to the next generation. Now, it's your turn to embrace mentoring.

A well-planned and supported mentoring program, backed by hard work, know-how, and resources, can have an impact year in and year out. It goes a long way toward helping you develop, engage, and retain your people. Once the program has gained momentum, it can instill a culture of mentoring for professional development in your organization. If done well, it will delight your participants and stakeholders.

While it is no easy task to build a mentoring program from scratch, by following our Seven-Step Process, you will successfully achieve your mentoring goals and strengthen your organization. The best way to achieve a good result is to think carefully about what mentoring you're going to provide, how you're going to deliver it, and how you can evaluate it to make it even better.

✓ Success Secret: Get started on these seven steps to create your high-impact mentoring program!

As Zig Ziglar said, "You don't have to be great to start. But you have to start to be great."

Aristotle. *The Nicomachean Ethics.* edited by Lesley Brown and David Ross, Oxford University Press, 2009.
Maxwell, John C. *Developing the Leader Within You.* Thomas Nelson Publishing, 2012.

CHAPTER 16

Bonus Chapter: The Case for Virtual Mentoring— Tips for Mentors, Mentees, and Program Managers

In traditional mentoring relationships, the mentor and mentee interact face-to-face. Yet, like all relationships, mentor-mentee interactions are evolving. Remote mentoring is a flexible, effective alternative to in-person mentoring experiences for online students and remote employees who are part of a global workforce or are working from home for other reasons.

While I believe in-person meetings build relationships quickly and are most effective for mentees, they are not the only way to connect. We learned this during the worldwide COVID-19 pandemic in 2020.

Meaningful mentoring relationships can flourish through calls, video chats, text messaging, and other virtual forms of conversation.

Of course, as with traditional mentoring, careful planning and intentional communication continue to be vital.

First, let's discuss the benefits and challenges of virtual mentoring; then we'll go into some guidelines on how to make your efforts successful.

Benefits

Virtual mentoring has many benefits—chief among them:

- **Larger Pool of Mentors.** Forward-thinking global organizations have already learned the value of being able to communicate any time virtually and from any place in the world, giving their employees access to a larger pool of mentors within their international organizations or externally. In the same way, virtual mentoring allows alumni mentors who have relocated away from their alma mater to mentor students and creates opportunities for people in rural, distant locations to connect with a mentor whose preferred skills or experience may be difficult to find nearby.

- **Flexibility and Convenience.** Participants in virtual programs appreciate the flexibility and convenience of virtual mentoring. With the help of technology, mentors and mentees can agree upon a time to meet, which allows them to manage different time zones, heavy workloads, and even childcare duties. If a busy executive is eager to mentor but can meet only after "regular office hours," s/he can be matched with someone in a time zone that allows the mentor to participate after hours and the mentee to participate during his or her regular hours—a win-win for all.

- **A Trifecta Win for Employee Morale.** Emotional support is vital to help combat the loneliness and isolation some remote workers report. A virtual mentor can provide that support. In a *Forbes* interview, Janice Omadeke, CEO and founder of The Mentor Method, described a three-way win for organizations that invest in mentorship programs: "You're providing a safe space for them to discuss their feelings, you're connecting your talent to resources that build resiliency, and you're showing an investment in their development, which can offer peace of mind, personally and professionally." (Tarr)

But is virtual mentoring effective? The answer is yes—it absolutely can be effective.

Research presented to the Society of Academic and Research Surgery (Erridge et al.) shows that mentoring via real-time videoconferencing yields equivalent outcomes to in-person mentoring. Researchers conducted a systematic review of 66 research studies focused on the remote mentoring of surgeons. Their results suggest that mentoring via real-time videoconferencing is feasible and provides *some* equivalence to on-site mentoring in regards to clinical and educational outcomes. I emphasize "some" because face-to-face mentoring continues to be the most ideal.

Challenges

Virtual mentoring presents some communication challenges. For example:

- **Things get lost in translation or misinterpreted.** Face-to-face mentoring offers more information about mentor-mentee engagement than can be gathered with virtual communication. Methods like email, chats, and text messaging are especially prone to misunderstandings because facial expressions, nonverbal gestures, and body language are missing. Zoom, Skype, FaceTime, and similar technologies are perhaps a happy medium.
- **Communication preferences vary.** Some people find it difficult to build rapport using a telephone, teleconferencing,

email, or text. Some are more comfortable with the phone than a video conference call. Some prefer email because it gives them time to reflect and to think, while others enjoy the immediate response of texting or chatting via WhatsApp. Hint: Program managers who are setting up remote mentoring programs should ask a specific question about communication preferences on intake forms and use that information if possible when matching mentors and mentees.

- **Time zones can be tricky.** For example, if the mentor is based in Australia while the mentee is in the U.S., then finding common ground for meeting times is daunting but doable through negotiation and flexibility.

- **It's easier to "disappear."** Unlike face-to-face programs, where you see someone regularly in the hallway at work or when attending mentoring events, it's easier for one party to simply "disappear" during virtual mentoring. Time zones and technology are easy excuses. Remote programs should encourage participants to establish a specific plan around when they will communicate and how they will address missed meetings to keep the relationship on track. This plan should be established up front.

- **Technology brings its own tribulations.** When the technology we count on breaks down, frustration is inevitable! Again, intake forms can help by having mentors and mentees list preferred platforms as well as those that simply won't work for one reason or another.

Interestingly, there is some evidence that when mentors and mentees communicate in multiple ways, it leads to more engagement and a greater sense of connection. So, program managers can encourage virtual participants to come up with a blended plan using more than one communication method with confidence. A mix of monthly phone calls and emails with quarterly Zoom meetings might work when time zones are a big issue, for example.

Virtual Mentoring in a Crisis

Research shows that when mentors engage with mentees, those mentees form stronger emotional bonds to the organization, report higher job satisfaction, and perceive more significant support from the organization broadly. This may be especially important in times of crisis. In a *Harvard Business Review* article focused on social distancing during the COVID-19 pandemic of 2020, David G. Smith and W. Brad Johnson declared, "Facing an uncertain future, mentees—now more than ever—will leverage connections with mentors to lower anxiety, overcome imposter syndrome, and grasp hold of their mentor's hopeful vision of how they can not only weather the storm but continue to thrive in their careers." (Smith and Johnson)

In ordinary conditions, mentoring relationships tend to focus on professional development and career-building. Although those are important, the psychosocial functions—acceptance, affirmation, friendship, emotional support, reassurance—are especially valuable and vulnerable in uncertain times. Demonstrating emotional and social support could start with generous listening to understand the struggles and concerns brought about by the crisis and to acknowledge and validate those challenges and feelings.

When forced to work remotely, virtual employees and students can feel distracted and adrift. This makes mentoring programs more important than ever, because they provide an opportunity to build connections and to have candid conversations around personal struggles, perplexing business priorities, and beyond. Mentors and mentees can be valuable anchors for one another, helping develop approaches for dealing with challenges, as well as providing advice, perspective, and support.

"Virtually" the Same Principles Apply

Creating and managing virtual mentoring opportunities can be exciting and somewhat challenging. All mentorship programs—whether they are in-person, remote, or some hybrid—require the same fundamental approach. Best practices for virtual mentoring programs in the workplace or university mirror standard best practices for face-to-face mentoring programs—things we have covered in this book.

That said, here are **Seven Top Tips for Effective Virtual Mentoring** for mentors, mentees, and program managers.

#1: FOCUS ON CLARITY

Establish expectations. For a virtual mentoring program, it's essential to provide a framework to ensure that everyone involved—mentors and mentees alike—understands the expectations for the relationship. The program champion/manager should provide participants with guidelines on meeting frequency, mentorship duration, mentoring best practices, setting goals for the partnership, and other guidance. The program manager also bears the responsibility of defining the roles and responsibilities of mentors and mentees, such as who is responsible for scheduling meetings *and* who is responsible for getting a derailed relationship back on track. This needs to be crystal clear from the start. Hint: The program manager can be a resource to mentors or mentees when the relationship is failing.

Reinforce accountability. Participants need to respect the investment each party is making and take action on what both agree to do. Participant engagement can be more challenging with virtual programs because skipping a video call could seem less harmful than being a no-show for an in-person meeting, but in reality, it's just as bad and can allow one person to begin to disappear as discussed before. To ensure participation, and to give a little nudge to mentors and mentees when necessary, program managers should send reminders and supportive tips to participants regularly.

#2: GET A HANDLE ON TOOLS AND TECH

Try different communication options. Virtual mentoring means that mentors and mentees need to decide how they want to communicate. There are many options.

- Do you use video chat? If so, which platform?
- Is it okay to text? If so, when are the best times?
- Is email okay if it's something non-urgent?
- Are phone calls acceptable? What number is preferred?
- Can you agree on a response turnaround time when working in different time zones?

It's great that today's technology allows us to see one another's faces while we talk. But with so many options out there, you must figure out what will work for the two of you in this relationship. There is no one right technology tool to use. The key is that mentoring partners take time to make sure both are comfortable with the technology you will be using to connect.

I strongly suggest that participants use video conferencing for meetings between pairs whenever possible because so much communication is non-verbal. Some video conferencing software options for meetings include:

- Zoom
- BlueJeans Meetings
- Microsoft Teams
- GoToMeeting
- Cisco WebEx
- Join.me
- Zoho Meeting
- Google Meet
- Skype
- FaceTime

If possible, use an existing platform to make the process easy for participants. If the mentorship program is through a workplace, the tool used in the office is likely the best fit. At the University of West Florida, we are Google-based, and so all students have free access to Google Meet as well as Zoom. Mentees may be able to engage in a little reverse mentoring to help mentors who may not use these platforms.

Create a backup plan for tech issues. Mentors and mentees should have a backup plan in place in anticipation of inevitable technical difficulties. Decide in advance what you will use if the go-to platform for your virtual mentoring meeting fails. For example, if the video connection starts to lag on your laptop, use your phone for audio. Also, keep cell phone numbers handy, just in case video call connections go sideways. There are many forms of communication available today. Test technologies and be creative and intentional with your connection tools of choice. Write the backup plan in the early stages—ideally before you need it.

#3: BALANCE CONSISTENCY AND FLEXIBILITY

Aim to stay consistent... Whichever way participants choose to connect, consistency is key. I recommend pairs set a meeting schedule and stick to it! In my experience, a schedule gives each person something to look forward to and depend on—a big bonus in uncertain times. And, a schedule that is added to the calendar can be a good way to keep other work obligations from overtaking mentoring time.

...But allow for negotiations when needed. Establishing a schedule that works for both parties may involve some negotiations. Participants must figure out the best timing and the best medium(s) for meeting in a virtual environment, which may require some adjustments to work around childcare, eldercare, time zones, and other commitments. Be open to changing the schedule—and sticking to the new one.

Hint: Program managers should check in at appropriate times as a friendly reminder for mentees and mentors to have consistent meetings.

To maintain a successful mentoring relationship, embrace patience, flexibility, and understanding.

#4: COMMIT TO HONEST COMMUNICATION

Communicate, communicate, communicate! As with anything else, communicating with each other and being honest are important in a mentorship. Ideally, virtual partners will be matched based in part on their communication styles. Still, remote mentoring may require one party to move outside of their comfort zone and to try a mode of communication they typically might not use professionally. If the chosen communication platform or the meeting schedule isn't working, that should be discussed and resolved without embarrassment or recriminations.

Be intentional. Participants should discuss if they have what they need to communicate effectively remotely. Both parties should openly talk about what they need to maintain a vibrant relationship, especially if there are time zone differences. Participants in different time zones may decide, for example, that a combination of phone calls, emails, and Zoom chats makes good sense. Emails allow for a thoughtful response, and Zoom chats include the visual cues we discussed. Mentors can help turn this experience into a teachable moment on managing time in a virtual work environment and using new communication tools. Hint: Program managers for global business may need to take the lead with IT to make sure participants have the necessary hardware and software to support the virtual relationship envisioned.

Be forgiving. During high-stress times, people sometimes do and say uncharacteristic things. If your mentoring partner is working remotely during a time of crisis, be open to the fact that he or she may say things due to stress. Be flexible and understanding.

Don't get complacent. Because meeting online tends to feel a bit more casual, complacency can set in. Approach every meeting — whether it's video, phone, or text message — as if it's a formal meeting you'd have with a client. Both sides should come prepared. A good rule of thumb: Before the meeting, the mentee should send a brief agenda, even if it is as simple as one burning question. This simple act of professionalism can help set the tone (and it's a smart thing to do, whether you're meeting face-to-face or via technology like Zoom).

Pro tip: Be aware of mirroring. You will notice that if you write short, quick messages, you are more likely to receive short responses. So, if your virtual mentoring relationship relies on email, make sure to follow up on a rushed reply with a thoughtful "discussion." It's okay to tell your partner that you can't elaborate now, but you will later — as long as you consistently take the time for the follow-up.

Be considerate. Virtual mentoring enables you to easily connect with people in different cities, countries, and time zones. However, that doesn't mean you should send a text to your mentoring partner at 2:00 a.m. with a thought that popped into your head as you were trying to fall asleep. Be considerate of each other and discuss when the best times are for connecting — or agree in advance that it is not necessary to respond to texts and emails that come at odd hours. This consideration should also encompass any changes that need to occur because of a person's daily life situation. It may be a good idea to ask, "How is it going?" before getting into the meeting, with the understanding that a mentor or mentee is free to share a difficult situation in confidence—all the more important if remote work is imposed in a crisis.

Hint: If mentoring partners are working in different time zones, they may want to "translate" their partner's office hours to their time zone. For example, California is 16 hours behind Tokyo. If a mentee is in California, the most convenient time for a video chat with their mentor is probably between 5:00 p.m. and 6:00 p.m. In Tokyo, that translates to between 9:00 a.m. and 10:00 a.m., the next day.

Establish clear boundaries for the mentoring relationship. For example, a mentor may need to block off time when a major project deadline is coming up. Or, perhaps there's a work or family emergency or other reason that a participant can't meet their obligations to their match. In such cases, it's imperative to let the other know about that, so they don't feel that they've been abandoned. Effective communication helps ensure the success of the virtual mentoring relationship.

Don't be afraid to ask for feedback. Mentors and mentees need to ask for feedback from their mentoring partners along the way. It might seem like things are going wonderfully. Or so you think. How do you know? Ask for the feedback outright.

Program managers: Get proactive about helping. Going from strangers to trusted mentoring partners can be a bit more challenging when interactions take place virtually. Program managers can help by providing a list of conversation starters and potential questions a mentee can ask a mentor. Similarly, the program manager can provide mentors who don't know how to draw out a shy or introverted mentee with icebreaker questions and open-ended questions that will get their mentees talking and comfortable.

#5: WORK HARD TO STAY CONNECTED

Be real. Increase personal focus. When you're not physically together, there can be a tendency to become more tactical and overlook the vital upkeep of relationships. When task orientation increases, the feeling of belonging can diminish. If your face-to-face meetings used to be 10 percent personal and 90 percent professional, adjust that percentage to create the time for increased "personal" focus. But don't force it. Everyone is different. Some people appreciate the opportunity to talk about their personal situations, and others don't.

Be authentic. Mentors and mentees are in this mentoring relationship together. Work to give a sense of yourself; share things that are important to you at school, work, and in your personal life. If you have roommates or children at home, or if you are worried or sick, don't hide those obstacles. Use them to "keep it real" and to cultivate a solid connection with your match. Sharing your specific situation could make it more comfortable for your match to share theirs.

Be in the moment. Everyone knows you should minimize distractions during an in-person mentoring meeting, such as silencing your cell phone. It's just as, if not more, important to give your undivided attention to virtual mentoring conferences. Be fully present in the moment with your match. You may find there are distractions (think children, pets) when attempting to meet virtually. Let your coworkers, family, or roommates know you are going to be busy with your virtual meeting. Turn off or mute your phone, close all other programs on your computer, and turn off computer notifications. If you expect an interruption, mention it or consider rescheduling for a time when you can be more present.

Be compassionate. Make sure your mentoring match understands you care. Many of us go through life assuming that the people around us know we care about them. Why else would we do everything we do, right? In virtual mentoring, it's even more important to make sure people feel the care, not just hear the words. Try to show empathy when your mentoring match is facing a stressful situation. Is your mentee struggling with something at school that you thought had been fixed weeks ago? Is your mentor not readily accessible like they had been a couple of months before? The point of a mentoring relationship is for it to be a personal connection where you both learn, grow, share, and become better off as a result. Have patience with yourself and your mentoring partner when needed.

Acknowledge and address concerns. Listen well to hear your mentor match's concerns. Financial, health, job, school, and family matters can all be pressing issues. Demonstrate that you hear and understand; that helps validate your match's emotions and shows you care. That doesn't mean that you have to rescue or fix anything for your mentoring partner. In its place, offer support that will help them overcome challenges on their own. Provide resources, strategies, and skills that they can use to learn, grow, and succeed.

Maintain connection, trust, and confidentiality. Make sure your match knows that out of sight doesn't mean out of mind. Get to know your match as a person. Build trust with them by honoring your commitments and being accountable.

Don't skip the video conferencing. As I mentioned before, the mentor and mentee must have face time. Eye contact and nonverbal gestures serve as cues to both parties. It's critical to see the person from time to time so you can pick up on facial expressions and non-verbal cues.

#6: WHEN REVIEWING GOALS, REMEMBER, CHANGE HAPPENS

Be flexible. Having clear goals is a foundational piece of a mentoring relationship. However, with virtual mentoring, as with traditional mentoring and life itself, you need to be flexible and allow for some messiness. Depending on what is happening in someone's life or the world at large, allow time to chat about life before you shift your focus and dig into the mentoring goals.

If you find it takes a few exchanges before you can focus on professional development goals again, be kind to one another and have empathy for one another (and yourself!). You may find that you need to toss your original mentoring goals out the window and set new goals. You might find that you are using your virtual meetings to share fears, express challenges, and just talk in general on a human level. This is okay, completely normal, and can be extremely valuable to both mentee and mentor.

Adapt to a new environment. Many of us have experienced working remotely, either from home or while traveling for business. However, mentor participants who have been *forced* to work remotely might be experiencing mentoring virtually without the workstations, desks, phone equipment, and the IT support they usually rely on. Also, a participant could be sharing a workspace with other coworkers or children, or dealing with pets, parents, or roving roommates. All of this may force you to make adjustments to the frequency, timing, and structure of your virtual meetings. Tips to help: Do your best to find a private location for your "meetings," try to minimize the likelihood of background noise or disruptions, and use headphones instead of the computer speaker. It is essential to treat these meetings with the same confidentiality and courtesy as you would if you were meeting in person.

#7: EMPHASIZE COMMITMENT

Acknowledge the commitment. Engaging in a virtual mentoring relationship takes time and energy from everyone, but it is worth it. Before you begin your mentoring connection, think about how much time you have available to dedicate to a mentoring relationship and whether or not that matches the requirements of your mentoring program. For example, at the University of West

Florida, we expect mentors and mentees to "meet" at least once a month for an hour. They can certainly meet more often if it works for both parties. In other mentoring programs, mentees spend half an hour per week talking with their mentors. This doesn't sound like a lot, and it isn't, but it's easy to fall behind if your connection isn't a priority. Virtual mentoring is more susceptible to loss of commitment than face-to-face mentoring. So participants must acknowledge the time commitment—both for themselves and for their mentoring partner.

Ensure support from others. Make sure your colleagues, family, friends—whoever is around when you have your virtual meeting—understand what you're doing. If someone walks by and sees you on the phone or a video chat, it would be easy for them to assume the call isn't important. Alert people that this meeting is sacred and that you shouldn't be disturbed. Close your door if you can or seek out a quiet, private space where you can connect with your mentor/mentee in peace.

Don't end meetings early. It's easy when you're meeting remotely to end sessions early. Resist the temptation and stick to the prearranged time. If you leave one meeting early, it's easier to leave the next, and the next, early, and suddenly complacency sets in. If you've covered the agenda in less than an hour, return to your goals and see how you are doing.

You get out what you put in. I'm sure you've heard this before—and it's true. In my experience, when someone doesn't get what they need out of a mentoring connection, it's often because the relationship was not made a priority by one or both parties. Everyone has commitments and obligations, whether work or family or both, but it's vital to remember to set aside time for personal growth too. If you find that there is too much going on and it feels like you don't have a minute to spare, take a few deep breaths, and then explain to your mentoring partner what's going on.

From there, they can advise you on how to make things easier and provide support. Whatever the outcome, don't give up! It takes some time and patience to see results. Therefore, not giving up when tough times come—such as scheduling conflicts or not seeing immediate results—is necessary.

Keep Calm and Mentor On!

Virtual work or school environments are no reason to pause your professional development, including your mentoring relationships. It is the opposite. Remote mentoring can keep your connections active while still allowing for productive interactions between mentor and mentee. I have seen over and over again that being in a virtual mentoring relationship can be fulfilling, rewarding, and meaningful. If you have the opportunity to participate in virtual mentoring, use it as a chance to stay connected with colleagues, continue your growth in personal and professional development, and be a part of a mentoring movement that proves we are stronger and closer together—no matter how far apart we may be.

Erridge, Simon et al. "Telementoring of Surgeons: A Systematic Review." *Society of Academic and Research Surgery*, 2017.

Smith, David G. and W. Brad Johnson. "Social Distancing Doesn't Have to Disrupt Mentorship." *Harvard Business Review*, 2020.

Tarr, Tanya. "How Virtual Mentoring Is Closing the Loneliness Gap During COVID-19." *Forbes*, 2020.

ACKNOWLEDGMENTS

BERT THORNTON

My "I am grateful for…" list is far too long to publish here.

Some people, like Quint Studer, inspire me with their selfless gift of time and treasure to others, most of whom they don't even know and some they will never meet. Quint knows how I feel about him. It's a good idea to pay attention to anything he writes or says.

Ironically, there are many others who have been surprised to learn they have unknowingly inspired me. I'm always dismayed at folks who have such a great deal to say and so much to share with others and just don't know it. You might be one of them. If you are, know you are appreciated by the people who benefit from your contact and interaction.

There are friends and family for whom I am grateful in the context of this book:

- Albert Thornton Sr.—perhaps the most honest man I ever met and forever inspirational
- Joe Rogers Jr.—who mentored me and gave me the chance to help build the iconic Waffle House culture
- Jim Rohn and Earl Nightingale—fathers of motivational speaking and early unknowing mentors to me

- My deep thanks go to several good friends and associates who took the time to read and advise on this book. Their advice to me has always been spot-on.
- Don Yaeger—eleven-time *New York Times* best-selling author
- Dr. G. Wayne Clough—author; president emeritus, Georgia Institute of Technology; secretary emeritus, Smithsonian Institution; and quoted in this book
- Sonny Perdue—former governor of Georgia; former United States Secretary of Agriculture
- Andrew Kilpatrick—author, *Of Permanent Value: The Story of Warren Buffett*
- Marti Walsh—senior marketing director at Fortune 500 companies
- Jean Marie Richardson—businesswoman; entrepreneur; founding CEO and president, iFOLIO
- Michelle Gallagher—director of community engagement, Delta Air Lines
- Mark Faulkner—president and CEO, Baptist Health Care in Pensacola, FL
- D.C. Reeves—author; businessman; chief entrepreneur officer, The Spring
- Rachael Gillette—president, Studer Community Institute
- Scott Remington—president and managing shareholder, Clark Partington Law Firm; and quoted in this book
- Katherine Kelbaugh, PhD—executive director, Museum School of Avondale Estates in DeKalb County, Georgia; executive director, National Association of Museum Schools
- Olevia McNally—an inspirational young businesswoman mentioned in this book; director, telemedicine practice development, Envision Physician Services
- J. Alistair McKenzie—Florida trial attorney; entrepreneur
- Pete Nowak—businessman; Pensacola-area McDonald's franchisee

- Heath Owens—Florida Gulf Coast businessman
- Devin Simmons—COO, TEC, Inc.; former CEO, Waterfront Rescue Mission, Pensacola
- Greg Hulett—Texas businessman who also helped me with *Find an Old Gorilla*
- Dave Rickell—executive vice president, operations, Waffle House; talented young man mentioned in this book
- Jim Hosseini—executive vice president, Waffle House; also played a very big part in the writing of *Find an Old Gorilla*
- Karen Head, PhD—professor, associate chair, and executive director of the Naugle Communication Center, Georgia Institute of Technology; editor of the international, award-winning poetry journal *Atlanta Review*
- Quint Studer—author; businessman; philanthropist; and…"the mentor's mentor"
- Sherry Hartnett, PhD—my immensely talented friend and colleague who was gracious enough to explain the challenges of and solutions for developing and driving a large and successful mentoring program in the big leagues
- Dottie DeHart—who kept it all together and brought the book to life

And especially, I am grateful for Kathy—my wife, my love, and my best friend.

DR. SHERRY HARTNETT

The world is a better place thanks to individuals who share their gift of time to mentor others. Thank you to everyone who helps others grow and develop.

To all the people I have had the opportunity to lead, be led by, or mentor throughout my career, I want to say thank you for being the inspiration and foundation for the Executive Mentor Program at the University of West Florida. I have been fortunate to have had many tremendous mentors throughout my life. I cannot tell you how much I appreciate your guidance and generosity. I wish I could name all of you individually.

I especially want to thank the friends, family, and colleagues who helped make this book possible. Thanks to Bert Thornton, mentor extraordinaire, for inviting me to coauthor this book with him.

Special thanks are due to those who gave their time to read or edit my manuscript, including Peggy Mika, Laura Swann, Pam Bilbrey, Michael Ryan, and Dottie DeHart. Your honesty, advice, and suggestions helped me refine my ideas and approach, and this book is richer for your contributions.

I am grateful to the innovative leaders at UWF who fully supported my vision for the Executive Mentor Program: Martha

Saunders, Judy Bense, George Ellenberg, Ed Ranelli, Tim O'Keefe, and Rick Fountain. I acknowledge and thank the hundreds of student mentees and business executive mentors who have participated and shared their stories through the years in the Executive Mentor Program, and team members who helped me create and guide the program: Rachel Hedrick, Katina Hoffman, Ana Carrasquillo, Charlene Holmes, and all of our fabulous work-study students and graduate assistants.

And finally, I thank my family, who encourages and supports me in so many ways: my parents, Ray and Marian, and sister, Holly, who have cheered me on throughout every step of life's journey. My gratitude also goes to my extended family, who are always caring and helpful, no matter how far away or busy they are…to my sons, Jake and Brad, who bring me the greatest joy and are an inspiration to me daily…and especially to my husband, Bob, for always being there for me and being my best friend.

Thank you, God, for everything.

BERT THORNTON

Bert Thornton is a 1968 graduate of the Georgia Institute of Technology, where he attended on a full football scholarship. He spent two years as an artillery officer in the United States Army, serving a tour with the 5th Battalion, 2nd Artillery in South Vietnam.

Upon separation from the service, Bert worked as a systems analyst and salesman in NCR's IT Division, and in 1971, he joined Waffle House as a manager trainee. Four years later, Bert became a vice president.

He spent 40 years shaping careers (including his own) as Waffle House grew from a few southern restaurants to the iconic national presence it enjoys today.

As president and chief operations officer, Bert felt his number-one priority was the development of quality leaders and leadership skills within the Waffle House management team.

In recent years, Bert has focused his message on emerging leaders from many other companies, educational institutions, and business associations. Thousands of students, mentors, and businesspeople of all ages have heard and benefited from his "Success Tactics" presentation and other talks covering many other subjects.

Bert is also very active at Georgia Tech, serving from 1996-2000 as a member of the Alumni Association Board of Trustees. In 1999, he chaired Tech's highly successful $7.8 million annual giving "Roll Call" initiative, and was named president of the Alumni Association in 2001 and 2002. He has been a member of the Georgia Tech Foundation Board of Trustees since 2001 where he has served on the Finance, Development, and Stewardship Committees. In 2016, Bert received the Joseph Mayo Pettit Distinguished Service Award, the highest award conferred by the Georgia Tech Alumni Association.

He is a member of the board of directors of the Studer Community Institute in Pensacola, Florida, and is an entrepreneur-in-residence at the University of West Florida Center for Entrepreneurship.

Bert also has an advisory board role with the Museum School of Avondale Estates, an award-winning charter public elementary-middle school in DeKalb County, Georgia. He is a former trustee of the school and was honorary chair for the Museum School's successful $5 million expansion capital campaign.

Bert's first book, *Find an Old Gorilla: Pathways Through the Jungle of Business and Life,* is a very well received leadership handbook for rising high achievers and emerging leaders.

Today, Bert is vice chairman emeritus of Waffle House, Inc., the largest full-service, sit-down, 24-hour restaurant chain in the world.

And, if you are a Waffle House fan, yes, he is the Bert of Bert's Chili.

To learn more about Bert, please visit
www.highimpactmentoringbook.com.

Order Your Copy of Bert's First Book, *Find an Old Gorilla: Pathways Through the Jungle of Business and Life*

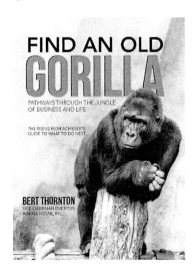

If you wake up one morning and realize you have to travel through a jungle, it would make sense for you to find an "old gorilla" and take him or her along. The "old gorillas" are the ones who know where all the good pathways are—as well as the quicksand that can bring you down. With *Find an Old Gorilla: Pathways Through the Jungle of Business and Life*, Bert Thornton stakes his claim as one of these wise and seasoned guides. The vice chairman emeritus of Waffle House Inc., Bert joined the company as a manager trainee and helped it become an iconic restaurant chain, retiring as its president and chief operations officer.

Find an Old Gorilla is the rising high achiever's guide to what to do next. In it, Bert shares how to use basic techniques to effectively focus on business and life success, evaluate and confront problems in an orderly fashion, find and work with the right mentor at the right time, follow time-proven Basic Laws of Success, and capitalize on the strategies and secrets of effective leadership.

Filled with advice and practical strategies, this emerging leader's handbook is the precursor and perfect companion to *High-Impact Mentoring*. If you are a mentor, you may want two copies of *Find an Old Gorilla*: one for you and one for your mentee. And if you run a mentoring program or are hiring Bert to speak to your organization or group, please consider ordering multiple copies for a bulk discount.

Please visit www.highimpactmentoringbook.com to learn more.

DR. SHERRY HARTNETT

Dr. Sherry Hartnett is a highly respected marketing and leadership professor, consultant, and mentor. She entered the world of academia after a successful business career as a senior-level marketing executive. At the University of West Florida, she founded the pioneering, high-impact experiential learning Executive Mentor Program and an acclaimed annual Women in Leadership Conference to educate the next generation of business leaders who will shape the destiny of our future.

Sherry founded Hartnett Marketing Solutions and Hartnett Learning Academy, a consultancy specializing in marketing and leadership development. Before launching her consulting company, she was vice president, chief marketing and development officer at a regional healthcare system recognized as a Malcolm Baldrige National Quality Award winner and one of Fortune's 100 Best Places to Work. Earlier in her career, Sherry was a marketing executive for one of the top ten largest news media companies globally, and led marketing and research for a national advertising agency.

Sherry has a unique perspective on leadership that shines through in her writing on the importance of mentorship. Sherry has received numerous national awards and honors for excellence in marketing, leadership, and mentoring and prestigious faculty excellence in teaching awards. She is delighted to see her students and clients prosper and flourish. Sherry is always looking to inspire and encourage others and has served as a mentor to many.

An active leader in business, civic, and charitable communities, Sherry has served on numerous national and local boards of directors over the years, including the American Marketing Association and the Pace Center for Girls Escambia-Santa Rosa, as board chair for Junior Achievement of Northwest Florida, and as president of the Rotary Club of Pensacola. She is also a proud member of the Leadership Florida Cornerstone Class 38.

A lifelong learner, Sherry received a bachelor's in marketing from Towson University, a master's from Johns Hopkins University in management, and a doctorate in business from Georgia State University, and is always on the lookout for fascinating and relevant things to learn.

Sherry is well known for her energetic and interactive teaching style and for providing advice and guidance that is down-to-earth and relevant, and that takes into account the real-world complexities of business. She has a passion for making a difference in the careers and lives of the next generation, locally and worldwide.

Sherry and her husband are the proud parents of two grown sons and reside in Pensacola, Florida.

Find out more about Sherry at www.sherryhartnett.com

Continue Your Mentoring Journey
with an online course

There has never been a better time to take your leadership and organization to a whole new level through high-impact mentoring.

As a complement to this *High-Impact Mentoring: A Practical Guide to Creating Value in Other People's Lives* book, the **High-Impact Mentoring** online course leads you through the process of implementing a mentoring program at your business or organization. Sometimes showing, not telling, is more valuable. The course includes case studies to illustrate book content, with visuals of mentoring program branding materials, applications, commitment forms, and more.

The **High-Impact Mentoring** course is filled with checklists, proven strategies, a tool kit of downloadable PDFs, and specific resources to help implement your program.

Sign up for the course:
www.highimpactmentoringcourse.com

Access additional resources: www.hartnettacademy.com

SherryHartnett.com

LinkedIn.com/in/sherryhartnett

HartnettAcademy.com

Need Additional Copies of
High-Impact Mentoring?

Of Course You Do!

We hope you've enjoyed our book. It occurred to us you might want to share it with current and future mentors and mentees, leaders, and/or others who may be interested in starting a mentoring program. When the whole organization embarks on a journey together, a successful outcome is far more likely!

You might also have friends, family members, or colleagues outside your organization who would benefit from the book.

For all of these reasons, we're offering bulk discounts when you order multiple copies of *High-Impact Mentoring*. (The more you order, the more you save!)

For details, please visit www.highimpactmentoringbook.com.

Thank you so much. We are grateful to all who share the gift of mentoring with the world!

—Bert Thornton

—Dr. Sherry Hartnett